My Soul Sings

Poetry in Spare Time

Volume One

Gossie Harold Hudson, Ph.D.

GATEWAY PRESS, INC.
Baltimore, MD   2003

First Printing, Baltimore, 1999
Second Printing, Baltimore, 2003

Please direct all correspondence and book orders to:
Mrs. Florence D. Hudson, Director
The McCall Research Corporation
1020 E. Belvedere Ave.
Baltimore, MD 21212

Library of Congress Control Number 98-75582
ISBN 1-893574-01-6

Published for The McCall Research Corporation by
Gateway Press, Inc.
1001 N. Calvert Street
Baltimore, Maryland 21202-3897

Printed in the United States of America

Dedication

First, thanks to my wife,
Mrs. Florence Delories (McCall) Hudson
for all the inspiration and motivation
and hard work in helping me to become
what I am, then

For My Children —

Casandra, Gossie, Jr., Florence,

And Theirs:

Erica, Melvin, Lindsay

Keith

Justin

FLORENCE

Contents

v

Foreword

Gossie's poems could not be more aptly named— "My Soul Sings". For that is exactly what they are—poignantly, searching expressions which reflect the thoughts of the writer relative to heritage, color, civil rights, folklore, comedy, religion, genealogy, sensitivity, commitment, and the deeper strivings, struggles, and aspirations of this historian/poet/teacher who also happens to be a musician. Their charm, along with information, humor, vitality, and frequent bawdiness from poem to poem, will have the reader eagerly moving from one page to another in order to find out what comes next. This first collection is full of his warm, creative soul and is always surrounded with wit and wisdom.

Gossie Harold Hudson was born in New Bern, North Carolina, the only child of Bertha Elizabeth and Gossie Mack Hudson, his first teachers. Following his public education in New Bern, he attended what is now Morgan State University in Baltimore, Maryland. His stint in the Army during the Korean Conflict confirmed to him that he could not tolerate regiment and petty discipline. However, it gave him the opportunity to see other parts of the world, embrace new languages, and find his unique niche in life—teaching. Following his military service, Gossie taught public school, played his horn in numerous, nameless night clubs, and eventually returned to academe. He earned the Ph.D. degree from Ohio State University, where he combined his love of history and poetry in his discovery of Paul Laurence Dunbar, his poetic forebear, Dr. Hudson is a tenured professor of history at Morgan State University, where he daily indulges his many interests. He is truly a Renaissance Man of the modem era who excels in diverse disciplines.

The many moods and faces of Gossie can be seen in these verses. Some of them are insightful, others angry, while others still are outrageously funny ("Cars in Charm City"), whimsical, or romantic. The works of this unapologetical African-American man strike a chord in the memories of those with whom he shares experiences—love, wonder, enslavement, addiction, emancipation, respect, trust—all of those qualities which make up a human being. Leap into the world of Gossie as you turn these pages, and it is guaranteed that you will see parts of you and your world too.

It will soon be obvious to the reader that Gossie does not follow the traditional rules of poetry, whatever they may be. His works are open and submit only to his style. Some of them rhyme, many do not; some use capitalization and punctuation, many do not; some are quite lengthy, others are as brief as 4 or 6 lines. He often uses punctuation marks as if they are words, intended to evoke a question, express amazement, or note the unthinkable. He is a highly educated historian who knows the language well; therefore, what may appear to the uninitiated to be incorrect grammar or misspelled words, is actually his way of extending his thoughts with unorthodox ellipses, commas, and dashes.

In some of his more serious poems ("I, Teacher", "Old Sycamore") he includes the thoughts or experiences which inspired him to write the poem. Many of the poems are dedicated to someone with whom he has interacted or whose memory he cherishes. Still others have near epic quality ("Sunday Morning", "No Ordinary Man, Uncle Wilson") as he tells a story which may be funny or poignant, but always a story with an underlying message.

Finally, the historian in Gossie wants always to leave a record. He dates and indicates the time of day he wrote many of his poems, a study of which gives some insight into his highly unconventional lifestyle. Those who venture into his world quickly learn that neither clock nor calendar governs Gossie's creative juices.

And now, the poems!

— Amy Powell, Editor
Baltimore, 1997

Introduction

What can I say about me or my poetry? It's just me, now for all the world to see. I struggled for many years to put my thoughts down on paper, to record what I see and feel and think and hear. And for years I did just that: I wrote on big yellow pads, on napkins, on the backs of programs, on my course syllabi, on the wall (sometimes) so I wouldn't forget. But I rarely showed these little ditties to anyone because I was afraid of criticism. But a few years ago a friend convinced me that these poems ought to be collected in an organized way before I leave this earth. That put the whole thing in perspective and I took a good look at my writings and fina plunged in. However, it took over six years and several false starts to finally put this book together. In trying to describe what I write, the best way I could do this was with a poem:

Poetry in Sparetime

I guess "Sparetime"'ll do it
Although I'll write a poem
Anytime one comes to mind
Whether 3 O'clock in the morning
Or 6 O'clock in the afternoon
I really don't care.
All of this means
That—in the bathroom
at the barbershop or in the train station
I'll even scribble out a few pieces
On a plane or on the way D.C. in a car.
I'm a poet, a writer
Who tells his life story in poetry
Whenever a few verses come to mind.
Maybe, then, the title of this book
Ought to be, "all the time"
'Cause that's exactly when I write:
every little chance I get—
anywhere and anytime!
A verse or two comes to mind.

— Gossie Harold Hudson
Baltimore, 1997

Black

(To Dr. James Emanuel,
nationally acclaimed Black poet)
July 21, 1983 - 1:30 p.m.

Black is the God who made me
Black the father who made me a He
Black is the woman who bore me
Black the struggle which set me free
Black is the nail I first stepped on
Black the hand that dried my tears
Black is the first gal I ever noticed
Black the burdens of the years
Black is the soul on the inside of me
Black the mind of my destiny.
Black is the detour through the pain
Black the ships of the Middle Passage
Black is the cross for a nation's rise
Black the way a hero dies.
Black is my head
And Black my feet
Black my awake
And Black my sleep
Black is the wind
Blowing Black to and fro
Black I come
And Black I go!

FENCES

Life is full
of fences/
They always
seem to
get in the
way/
I tried to
jump over
a fence
the other
day/ but
it was too
high;
too high
for me, that
Is!
All my
days
I've been
dodging fences/
little fences

BIG FENCES
white fences
yellow FEnces
nigger FEnces
colored Fences
negro FENces
Black FENCEs
FENCES!
I keep turning corners
ducking in Alleys
missing cars
but always
Fences!
One of these days
I gon git
ma knife AND
Ma iron
and cut-up
And shoot down
Some of them
Damn FENCES

MEMORIES
(Dedicated to the Class of 1949)

I remember it well—
the glory and charm of
youth;
the endless motivation
to learn, to dream—
And the strange feelings
of ambition and thoughts
of an illimitable,
uncertain world
that lay ahead;
But we were ready for it
or thought we were—
We said it often enough:
"Tonight we launch
Where shall we anchor?"
I remember—
Those days when Spring
Filled the air
Or rain filled-up my shoes
And the silly giggles, too—
We teased in the corridors
and hall/ways

Where we changed classes
As we splattered
Our infectious laughter
All over the place;
Those days when love
Pervaded the atmosphere
And our teachers
Caught/up in its magic
Never, really disciplined
us—
They couldn't/
They loved us only too
well!
Those days when
holding/hands
Was a monumental joy.
And stealing kisses
Was the height
Of all our devilment.
Those were the good ole
days
Those were the fond
years—
And I remember them
well!

The Blues
September 10, 1990 - 8:40 p.m.

I get-the/blues—so bad—sometimes
Nobody's shoulders
    to cry-on
It gets so-lonesome/
    Sometimes I need
Just a friend to/say hi
Or an enemy to/yell bye
would make me win,
    every now and then.
Just a little love
    A touch
    A hug
Perhaps a message
    I can identify with helps
        Sometimes/.

Often I'm devastated
Unless I pull somebody up
And share
    those blues,
    I need to lose.
But as I seem to hold
These funky blues—
I must understand
Life holds debts
For us to pay
In order to live well—
    everyday.

I guess I'll just pay
    Ma hard-earned dues
And be happy 'N free
    That's for me!
    No dues
    No blues.

4

On the First day of spring

On the first day of spring
I told a lady
It was gonna get cold again
She said, when? Because
This is the time
For the robin to sing—
Dresses to get shorter
And the days to get longer—
To go fishing. Time to slumber.
It's spring, it's spring
Good for my soul;
Let's sing, let's dance, and
"Let the good times roll!"

Las Vegas Strip
(New Orleans Time)

I thought this was it—
the alternative to
Bourbon street/WHITE Bourbon street
That is until I saw that roach crawling down on me—
until I saw that
White man
at the cash register counting that dough I had spent—
that other black folks had spent,
Maybe this wasn't IT after all
maybe this was only part of the game
of making us feel good
with all those discos and pretty "phat" Black women.
So we went on back
to Bourbon street and
dug Fat's Domino's son—Antoine
sing Blue Monday,
and saw those girls,
who were really boys,
and saw those white girls
wiggling and shaking
and showing those
naked bodies
and heard those Barkers
singing: "COME ON IN!"
(for the orgie, I guess),
and saw that dummy
swinging out that window—
And so we swung wid/it
and picked up a Hurricane at Pat O'Brien's
and split/

"One Brick Builds The Temple"
Nov. 16, 1994 - 11:17 a.m.

The Temple was magnificent
Sturdy and firm
A lesson in architecture
We all need to learn;
And so we asked the builder—
How was it all possible
This grandiose edifice
Of which we marveled?
His response was quick
Full of wisdom and wit
He scratched his grey head
And this is what he said:
He never could have done it
Without each brick along—
That's when we secured the mortar for each
And every individual stone-,
And sooner than we thought
A foundation took place
And before we knew it
A temple was right in our face.
How did we do it?
You've already guessed.
T'was really nothing to it.
We prayed and were blessed,
And that's how we did it—
One brick every day
With God leading the way
And, now our future's assured,
Each brick "one day at a time"
Makes a temple here to stay
Because no bricks were left behind!

On The Roof

The Rooftop
    in the city is
    a place to play—
    to take dares;
a place to get away
from the funky smell
    in the city's
        Row/houses
        and elevators,
        and nasty old car/lots
        in the projects.
Maybe a good/place
to drop a cat—
a friend,
or perhaps one's self/
even a place
to/share
        the terrible burden
        of being lonely,
or maybe a place
to hear good news,
or perhaps to find/out
        just how beautiful
        the inner-you can/be
        when you get/away
        from the humdrum-
        noisy beat
        of the city
        long enough
        to/discover
        the real you.

The Porsche Shop
March 1, 1979 - 2:00 p.m.

A Friend took me
by a Porsche shop
to purchase a part
that was/nt in?
Anyway—while
my feet ached and
my stomach shook
from dreams
of hamburgers and chicken
that by now
it looked like I was'nt
never gon git
I saw a pale/looking
white male
stan-ing on the
other side of the counter
looking just like Jesus
so I just went on/over
there—touched him
on his back and said:
"What's up—J.C.?"
and he got mad/n a mother/fucker,
Imagine!

Older Men
10-16-1992 / 12:50

I should think that if I were a woman
I would want an older man to/share
My life with because they seem
So courteous and respectful and
Always know just what to say and
The right word to use. But I
Don't think that I would ever really
Want to live with one because
I've got a sneaking suspicion—
Way/down deep inside of me— that once
I got one of those old fossils
Riled up he might be the meanest
Man in town!

Having Fun
3-8-96 - 9:13 a.m.

Folks in the city
like to have fun
playing with cars?
    Sometimes, they stick their foot out
        then jerk it back
        real quick
    Sometimes they make a run for it.
        Usually they beat the car coming
        just in time.
    Sometimes they dodge in and out
        between cars, and then
        jump out of "harms way"
    (Incidentally, drivers
    like to play, too. Don't believe it?
    Just let a police car siren go off.
    Everybody moves to the side—
    of course;
    but just as soon as the police cars
    pass, then comes the race
    through stop lights and stop signs
    for first place!)
But back to Homeboy!
I remember
the other afternoon when
Homeboy had donned his exercise
suit, cause he was going to show
those damn smart alec-ky
drivers "where it wuz at?"
Homeboy
had just finished a science course
at the local college
and he was thinking scientifically?
Homeboy
had figured this thing out—

11

if the driver was going 20 miles an hour
maybe even 25
there was a chance
his plan might work.
Having judged the on-coming car
Homeboy knew that he had time
to walk out in front of the driver
and move slowly; but also just fast enough
for the car to miss him, the only thing was—
that Homeboy had misjudged
the man's speeding car. Completely!
Pity!
For instead of 20 miles
the speedometer was on 40 and
the speed had increased considerably
by the time it reached Homeboy.
When Homeboy came down from the sky
about a block beyond the mishap
he fell on two more
"game-players" trying to dodge cars—
he busted their heads, broke their legs
And all three of them fell in front
of another car which hit them
in the rear of their hind parts.
Homeboy got up
wiped the blood from his head and body
dusted himself off and yelled out that
"something ought to be done
about these-here reckless drivers in the city.
When the PO-lice-man came
They took a quick reconnaissance of the situation
took-out his Billy club whipped Homeboy's tail
and took him to jail—
end of games for the DAY!

Birds

(My first poem—written when I was in the 8th grade,
West Street high School, New Bern, N.C.)

Birds are wonderful things to see
They never fight like you and me
They chirp and chirp and chirp all day
They never fight they always play.

They gather grasses for their nests
So they will have a place to rest
And that is why we shouldn't shoot them with guns
But build them bird houses and feed them crumbs.

Song of Service
(For Ushers)

I will wait for my change
No matter what it takes,
For God will forgive me—
He looks past my mistakes.

I will serve—thee, God
Whatever comes
I will follow you.

Though the winds—blow hard
I shall carry on
In the name of God.

My call—is sure
My faith is pure
I'll serve God—
As a loving steward.

I will stand on the "wall"
By God's grace
I will not fall
Until my Savior Calls—
            Me/home.

Dear "Candy"

A poem especially for my daughter,
my buddy, my friend
Written July, 1997

Ma heart leaped up/when I saw you last!
I guess because I care, about your past.
Maybe it's just our way, in N.A.
To know what's going on with somebody else
And say just the right thing that helps them
AND my/self That's the miracle that's
The message. Folks say some
Of-us go through the fire and come
Out as pure gold. That sounds good.
Maybe it's true. I don't know? I do know
That holding/on in spite of—seems to-be
The right idea because the rainbow
Seems to appear after the rain. After all,
God did create light out of darkness.
"Walk Tall," sister, "Keep your chin up" and
Remember—you're never alone, NA
Is with you. I—am with you and the
Message is always there for us both
To/share. It's in the song. It's in the
Wind. Listen to the singer and dream
Good dreams/about yourself It's so
Simple: "Jesus Savior, pilot me
Over life's tempestuous sea; unknown
Waves before me roll, hiding rock
And treacherous shoal; chart and compass
Come from Thee; Jesus, Savior, pilot me."
In other words, my dear sister—
God is still/
On His throne!

DISCOVERY

God's grace
Allows me to be—
A force of nature
with the ability to accomplish miracles.
That makes me spiritual then creative—
and in all this
I achieve self-acceptance
I know now why I exist—
to share love and happiness
With the world through the divinity
He allows me.\

I, TEACHER

Dedicated to my living teachers of West Street High School, New Bern, North Carolina: Mrs. Arabelle Bryant, Mrs. Blanche Rivers, Mrs. Lauretta Smith; Mrs. Evans; and to my greatest inspiration, the late Mr. Leon A. Mizell (Musician, Band Director, History Teacher)

Thoughts   7-15-92   6:30 p.m.

In my reflections, introspectively, I know of five men (all have passed from labor to reward) whom I have admired above all others: first of all Mr. Leon A. Mizell, my first, real inspiration; Mr. Frank Baker, history teacher; Dr. Earl E. Thorpe, author/historian and my mentor; Malcolm X; and Dr. Martin Luther King, Jr. Each of their lives has impacted on my philosophy and mindset in a uniquely, profound, and tremendous way.

I especially admired Malcolm and Dr. King for their brilliant wit and eloquence. There is one of King's speeches I shall never forget. It was about man's greatness. Dr. King said God made man great—made him in his own image and then he crowned him with glory and honor. You can bring man down in his wretched old age so that he can hardly walk and his vision is gone. But he takes his mind's eye and breaks through time and space and imagines that he hears the very angels singing and he comes back- his name is Handel, and he scratches across the pages of history, "A Hallelujah Chorus". You can't hold man down, man is great.

Yes man IS great. But most of all, man can be a teacher and only a teacher can do what no other human, in any vocational endeavor on this planet, can do. A teacher can cultivate and mold God's handiwork—the brain and the heart. And so it was with those thoughts that I wrote the poem following. I took my time composing it because herein lies the soul and the deeper strivings of Gossie. As a matter of fact, I decided when I was in the eighth grade that I wanted to be a teacher. I have never veered from that aspiration and that goal. At last—here is the poem.

I am the catalyst
God's charisma
The architect
Builder of minds
Creator of possibilities
The Motivator
Inspiring high hopes
Encouraging great leaders
The Master's helper

17

I, a teacher.
I transmit knowledge—
Culture and attitudes
Discipline and supervise
Influence and develop
I, a teacher.
I am many-sided, innovative
Knowledgeable, relevant
Challenging, informal
Instructive and patient
Serious and religious
Jovial and loquacious
I, a teacher- a tutor, a director.

I model and act
Initiate and communicate
I nurture the docile
Draw out ideas
Interpret to make aware
Develop mental powers
I indoctrinate
Explain and elucidate
I enlighten the mind.

I teach, I dread. I imagine?
I touch the potential
Reach through the impossible

Peep through the moon
Sky-dive in cosmic space
And play with moon beams
On a checker board of fate
I, a teacher.

I impart knowledge—
I urge my students
To dream beyond reality

Cross the Alps with Hannibal
Love knowledge for knowledge sake
Then remember
Their commitment to humanity
And the promises they must keep
That's teaching for me!
That's what I am.
I am what I saw in my teachers;
Perhaps my students—
God bless them, they
Will be what they see
In me
I am a teacher!

Counselors and friends
And well wishers
And Parents
And even teachers
select scientists
and doctors
and social workers
and mechanics
and preachers
and lawyers,
But God selects a Teacher.
Only a God
Can select the right person for the right mind
Only a God can do that!

A teacher's life is chosen.
He dwells among the Godly
His countenance is spiritual
And his place in Heaven is assured,
Because he alone
Can touch the brain of God.
The life of a teacher,
A REAL teacher—

19

Is Godly!
All of us wanted to/be something
In the forties—
I even thought I could draw—
(That thought didn't last too long)
I soon settled down to one dream,
I wanted to be a teacher,
It was a dream I couldn't shake,
God, am I glad of that!

We had some giant potential in my class—
Giants of science and engineering.
Businessmen and preachers
Musicians and photographers,
Social Workers and Administrators,
Counselors and Beauticians
Athletes and Cops.
School Teachers and Lawyers—
We had it all!

What I choose was teaching-,
And here I am—many years later
Still molding God's handiwork-,
The "Mind"
A dream since 19/forty nine—

REALIZED!

DAYBREAK ON THE ROAD
April 12, 1993 - 10: 10 p.m.

I wish I knew how to describe the sun when all of a sudden it
Pops up and you look through those bloodshot eyes and
   somehow see
That light—almost blinding...when you look, long enough—
makes you Shout, "God, man, it's daybreak." That's how it use
to be when I'd travel
Up and down those country roads from one gig to another
   with my
Sax between my legs talking about the next gig, or how glad
   I was
That God gave me the talent to blow my horn (and I could
   really
Blow that thing, man.) But back to that sun, that would
   always catch
Me unaware's. Sometimes I'd even try and stay awake long
Enough to actually see the sun-rise, but I'd always miss it.
   The booze
In my eyes would always let me down and I'd fall fast asleep
Thank God! It is not that way today, man!

FREEDOM NOW OR YESTERDAY

Birds have it, they fly where they want to!
No nest restrictions.
Trees have it, their leaves blow freely!
No wind directions.
White folks have it, they do what they want to!
No societal encumbrances.
Jews have it, they spend where they want to!
No economic hindrances.
And now I want it, I'm tired of the promises!
No more jiving.
I want my freedom, I'm damn tired of waiting!
No more denying!!!!

A POEM FOR OCTOBER
Columbus Day, In the U.S.A.

August 20, 1992; 10:00 p.m.

More than 2,000/years ago
Africans came to America's shore
They planted the cotton
They cut the corn
And they did all of this
Before Columbus was born
They built the Pyramids, observed the stars
Traveled afar and came to AmeriKA.
Columbus Day's a myth
School kids must know—
That Africans were first
They were here before/
Columbus came late
Get the story straight
Then put in the books
The facts of late—
That Africans discovered it
And brought in the light,
For America to see
Let's tell it right!

My Man
April 6, 1996 - 11:30 a.m.

Thanks MAN
for just being there for-me.
When the way seemed unclear
you crashed right through the darkness
and brought me a shining light
that showed me the SUN
at the end of the tunnel.
That gave me hope, MAN, and
that same hope sustains me, now
down through the winter years
       of my life.
Thank you SIR,
Thank you MAN.
Thank's!

Unity Nation

My heritage is at stake
Therefore, whatever it takes
I will resist all injustice
All white Anglo Saxon snobbery
All vestiges of white/Black bourgoesie behavior
And all other squelching elements/of
Funky racism—
With the strength of a mighty warrior—
    The African giant of my past!

Black Is Beautiful?

Wel-l-l—...?
Since Black Folk—
Brothers and Sisters
wear long hair
      long braided hair
      false hair
      slick hair
      curly hair
      blond hair
      brunette hair
      blow hair
      wavy hair
      plati-num hair
      straight hair
      pony tail hair
      "That Girl" hair
and act jest-lak
      white-folks
Whatever happened ta
Black is Beautiful?

KEEP THE FAITH

7-18-1997: 3:55 am
Written especially for my daughter,
Ms. Florence Elizabeth McPherson
(Candy)

Seems like only yes-
       terday
When you were enviably young
and gay—and so affectatiously carefree-
    and loquacious and talk-
ative, and laugh-
       ing and so eager to learn every-
           thing;
So inquisitive and vivacious
and smil-
   ing
everywhere we went
      Yes, those were the days;
the times when your hair always seemed
effervescent and
   Flow-
     ing, and your eyes were glaring
with anticipation of a bright future; and
we thought your college days
would change your ways
      and mine too,
perhaps?
    And it did happen for a moment,
but only like Omar Khayyam's snow
on the dusty earth—lighting,
for a little hour or two, and gone/
Oh where did all the time go—
how quickly the days
      turned into months
And the months into years.
      and now—

there you are,
                    And here am I—
dream—
          ing
about those impressive years
when you thought you'd never grow
up
      but you did, and
I'd give a million bucks
If I could just turn back the hands of time
and be the father
                    I should have
                                    Been,
but that thought soon perishes
when I perceive you
                    in the midst
of reality
          and realize that
God's grace
          will do for you
what IT did for me—grant you
Freedom—
          hope and faith—
                                    Peace and Love
At Last!

Grace
Good Friday, April 1, 1994 - 10:56 a.m.

Dear God:
   Whatever malady or mishap;
   Whatever physical impairment
      or mental disability—
   Whatever handicaps or encumbrances;
   Whatever "Jackpots" or squelchering
      circumstances
God, whatever...?
      Spare my Intellect!

HURT
(You ain't gonna like this poem)
December 14, 1994 - 8:13 a.m.

Hey Man!

You ever been hurt, I mean really HURT?
Ya'll ever had the blues?

Way down deep in your soul
in your groin
And in yo feet
When your baby's
Done gone and left-ya? Huh!

You know—I'm a Christian man
And a moral, ethical, intelligent man;
And I try to do the right thing
And say the right thing
And be the right thing
And put all round pegs in round holes
And sing all the right songs because
I'm logical and unemotional

BUT!

Woke up this morning—
And in the place where she lay
Ma/baby had done split
She had gone away?
I ran out the house
Caught a arm full of plane—
Had to get from there
But it was the same in the air—
She weren't there—man?
And there was no mo song in my heart anywhere!
At that precise moment, I could have cared less
About anything—neither the plane I was
in, nor the atmosphere in which it glided—and
That went for the president of the United States,

Congress and the Supreme Court.
I did not care about Pan Africanism or Afrocentrism—
Eurocentrism or any other kind of "ism". And
As much as I was caught up in the Civil
Rights Struggle, I cared little about racism and
    injustice and
The Ku Klux Klan and skinheads meant
Nothing to me—and the same went for Mohammed
Jesus, Buddha, Confucius, the angels, the devil
The air—I just didn't care. My love—any
Kind of love whatsoever—had turned to hatred
Because the jewel I had treasured had tarnished
And was long gone, from now on! I hated Kwanazaa,
Hanukkah
and "Born Again" Christians, in that order—
The hatred of my baby's absence had cut deep down
    into
My soul and logic, and by the way I didn't like
Ethiopian braids either!
I didn't care about Africa nor Europe
Nor the rest of the continents. I hated
Jupiter and Mars, Comets and stars—
Starfish and whales; Stan and the Klan. The Right
Wingers
And the White citizen councils—crackers and
    rednecks,
Peckerwoods and ofays, Newt Gingrich
And bourbon, pot and grass, and coke and dope
Uppers and downers and James Brown.
I hated paddies and punks and Bill Clinton, my
Imagination soared. I cursed be-bop and hip-hop
The butterfly, the tootsie-roll-the blues, jazz
And Yardbird and Nat King Cole, "Lady Day"
Sassy and Dinah—in fact I damned everybody and
Everything in Heaven and on Earth. Finally/
I let out just exactly how I truly felt—
Then I got REAL and said the magic words:
Like, motherfuck the whole Goddamn Thang—
I just want my baby back
So my heart can SANG!

SPRING
March 20, 1991 - 11:15 p.m.

Spring is here—
Time for flowers
          and sunshine
          and birds singing
Green grass and crickets,
Short sleeve shirts
          and short pants
          skirts and all that;
Time to dream,
To touch the other side
          of the sky
Before you die.
Time to laugh
          and play/and smile
your troubles away
          and say:
"I feel good"
(But it's snowing
          viciously outside.)
It's Spring anyway—
Tomorrow's another day!

Vigilance
May 12, 1989

I had a rendezvous
    with destiny

So I took my ship-out
With a will to/succeed
    But I fell short
One meter from the mark.
    I stepped back
        Two/meters more
Observed the situation
    From the bridge
Made sail
Then set my rudders
Toward the sun
    Knowing that
    What I pursued at first
    Was at least,
    Possible.

At last
    I sailed
        another time
    Missed my mark
    by one/half meter,
    and again—
I stood/back on the bridge
And tried once more!
This time
    Mission accomplished.

WHAT WHITE FOLKS GIVE
9/20/78 - 9:00 p.m.

White folks
just don't give a shit!
They never give a shit!
Ever listen to white folks
real close
They really never give a shit.
But they give a Black!
They give a Black hell
They give a Black mace
in the face.
They give a Black the claps
and the herpes
They give a Black the "chair"
They give Black/up for lent.
But they always say
They don't give a shit!
What in the hell
do they mean; they don't give a shit!
What they really mean
is that whereas
They don't give a shit
They do give a Black—
They do give a Black—all us Blacks,
a very shitty deal!

IT'S WEIRD

Here I am sitt'n here

Between two gossiping broads

Talk'n 'bout nothing;

With all these bottles of wine

Hot beer and cigarette smoke

All around me assaulting my nostrils

While now and then

An old Hillbilly song

Reminds me of Bronco Billy or somebody—

While my stomach turns over and over!!

Gee, I want a drink bad, now

I wanna drink

Worse than Peter

Loved the Lord. Pray God

 I get the hell out of here quick!

Junior/Senior Prom, 1948-49
2-19-91 - 1:40 p.m.

I really looked forward to THAT—
It was the one big event of the year
for ole West Street High
and I could hardly wait to
grove my girlfriend,
she in that long flowery evening gown
with MY corsage on
I had paid five dollars for
pinned on her breast,
and me in my tuxedo, tails and all,
with a slick bow tie
and patent leathered shoes-on.
The fun of it all, though,
was the wild anticipation.
Here was going to be my big chance
to kiss the one I thought
I loved—my childhood sweetheart?
I could even smell the carnations
and the lilacs and the cheap perfume—
It was going to be another glamorous affair
when I'd get to play "middle-class"
and act like white folks.
Being a musician
what I looked forward to most of all
were those pretty little ballads
that made me feel like
I was walking on egg shells—
"For All We Know," "Again", "Tuxedo
Junction", "Little Brown Jug",
"I Love You Truly", "A Train" and
then ending with—"I'll Be Seeing You—
In All The Old Familiar Places—"

Anyhow we'd have a'pur-dee
ball—waltzing and two-stepp'n
all over the floor.
Every now and then I'd show-off by dancing
with one of my teachers;
and after the prom I'd take my girl
home and kiss her about a hundred times
and then it would be all over
until the Junior/Senior Prom
next year.

WALKING TALL
Dedicated to my protégé, a brilliant student,
Mrs. Christine Robertson
June 18, 1991

Yesterday
    She discovered Afrocentricity
Then with her mind ajar
        She learned of Africa
And the Solomons and Shebas
She saw
    From behind the masks
She wore.
Now she walks tall
        Toward the Sun
Carrying the Book of Life
In her head—for
she will never dread
A future-less
        Than sure-success!

Jimmy Mack
2-27-96 - 11:23 a.m.

"Hey—Jimmy Mack, when are you coming back—"
It's been a year now since
Jimmy Mack
left this earth for another HOME
Two in the brains and two in the heart—
I thought he'd taught his buddies
a lesson.
The other day
I felt kinda flighty
So I went on down to the turf
Where Jimmy Mack and his boys
used to hangout
And sure enough
there they were—
drinking wine, smoking reefers
touting
and looking for a package.
By the way—
Jimmy Mack did finally
get "that" package
and spent the MAN'S dough
for the last time.
Will his boys ever learn
that messing with fire
and live wire
will surely BURN?
Incidentally—
Jimmy Mack
Ain't coming back
he's making his HOME
ready for his boys on the corner—
that same corner where Jimmy Mack
got his "burner".

Winning
4-17-91 - 9:19

I try to win, but always lose

It seems,

Yet win or not I keep my dreams,

I do my part

And leave it to God, He'll fix my

Heart

     No matter how I feel

     I/know it's God's WILL!

You see, It's faith and hope

That helps me live, helps me to cope.

Behind the night

     I see the light

     and the means

To struggle

     I'll have my dreams!

Black Forever
2-1-96 - 9:20 p.m.

One of these old sweet days or nights
the road less traveled—like Robert Frost said—
Which leads to that "undiscovered country"
where all humans must go is going
to open up for me.
And all my troubles and everything else
are going to be over and done.
But I'll be here anyway
whenever you hear an alto saxophone play.
Look for me in every classroom you see
Count my steps to and from the library.
Whenever you see Black stamp collectors
Whenever people are dancing, joking
And living without drugs or drinks
Whenever men are whistling
Working, visiting the prisons
Wearing expensive perfumes
giving words of comfort to the depressed—
That's when you'll see me.
When you feel the presence of God
in everything you do
when green peanuts taste like T/Bone Steak.
When snow reminds you of elementary school
and when it rains you think of the one you love
When you've seen the making of a tornado
And when you've been to Israel
And New York.
When you know how to step as
Well as walk—
Know how to understand
As well as talk
That's when you'll find me
laughing in the shade
About the miracle God has made.

Find me in the struggle for justice
Look for me in the bell of freedom.
Whenever civil rights grace the day
That's when you'll find me
down freedom way.
Look for me everywhere
then—
Catch my smile in the rainbow
hear my talk, but watch my walk.
See me in Africa, among my people.
Feel me in the heritage of Black folk
everywhere in the diaspora
And then call my name,
Call it loud—Blessed.
Black, African—Man!
African/Man,—wrong or right,
Black as the night.
For all to see, and all to be
Ebonied Black for eternity.

White

White
is European
thinking that blk/folks
are beastly people
childish, immature/people
on Welfare getting fat off the
system of white Anglo-Saxon Protestantism;
people who walk through/
over/around black people
without ever recognizing
their visibility/
White
Is a Great Big Iceberg of Racism.

The Slave
11/11/1994 - 2:25 p.m.

Go Down—
   Mo-ses
Way-down
   In Egypt-land
Tell ole
Pharaoh
   Let/my, people
      GO!
Go down, Moses, way down
In Egypt/land
Tell ole—Pharaoh
   Let/my—people—GO!
It was'nt always this way—
   My enslavement, that is,
I remember when I built pyramids
   and astronomical observations
   and commanded great armies
   and ruled over multitudes.
I remember when I was the iron center of the ancient world
   and traveled to Europe and the Americas
      And Asia and Antarctica and New Zealand and Finland
   and left my gold in faraway places.
We could do all things, man, because we were
The creators of the whole human race, creators of
civilization
The creators of religion, creators of Christianity
The creators of mathematics, astronomy, aeronautics
The creators of art, creator of Greek philosophy
The creators of the alphabet, the discovers of medicine
Discovers of science, inventors of steel;
the first saviors of mankind, The world's earliest messiahs
The founding fathers of the church, the originators of paper;
The first Martyrs, the first Ethiopians
The first Egyptians, first Mesopotamians
The first East Indians, first Chinese

40

The first Indo-Chinese, first Hebrews
The first Moors, first Europeans
The first Greeks, first Romans
The first Britains and the first Americans
But for a moment—we dropped our guard
And they enslaved me, you see!
 because of greed and arrogance
 and because I did'nt pay attention
And yet-when you heard my chains rattle
I was singing: "Before I'd be your slave, I would
 die and go in my grave
 then go home to my Lord and be free."
So all the while they were "enslaving"
 I was busy beating the Tom-Tom drums
 of freedom, man—liberation
 You know—
For they enslaved my body—but never my mind
 you see
I had left "THAT" behind
 In Africa, my home.

Colors Bother Me
August 8, 1993 - 6:50

I could see the hate
 in his eyes
I could see the pain
 damn/near
He was one of those Black boys
Who could have passed easily
 if he really wanted to
With his blond hair.
I wondered why he spat so violently
On that white lady's car
While she was in it.
Maybe he really wanted to be white
 After all
But couldn't?

MY LITTLE BOY

Written on the Author's Birthday
February 22, 1976, in St. Louis, Missouri

I miss my little boy!
I miss
The fishing trips we didn't make
The boating trips I promised him
The camping party I missed
All the games he asked me to play
The football sets that I did not
help him put together
The hunting we planned to do
The chess game we never played
The card games I lost
The ping pong games
The horseback riding I did not teach him
The movie shows we never saw
The football games I went to sleep on
The baseballs I never bought
The counseling sessions we never had
The times I lost my temper when
I shouldn't have
The first time he left home
The tears he never saw me shed
The curse words I shouldn't have used
The holiday dinners I was too drunk to make
The kindness I refused to give
The love I just did not share—
Gee, I miss my little boy;
But, he's a MAN now!

PUPPETS
9-25-77

The puppeteers are at it again
Twisting our bodies
willy-nilly, in accordance to
their desires, and their wishes;
not considering why our
hearts sing so sadly.
And we as puppets totally
dependent upon the whims
and idiosyncrasies of the puppeteers
move, rather lazily
into the directions that
we are guided/

The puppeteers have many faces;
Southern, Northern, Eastern, Western
conservative, liberal, moderate, democrat
strict constructionist, REPUBLICAN—
but they are all racists
all are haters of justice
all have the same goal
and the same task—
to make certain
that white supremacy never dies/

And so the puppets move,
rather lazily
into the paths...

Cars in Charm City
March 21, 1993 - 11:59 (morning)

I mean—cars will run-over-you
In BAL/tee-Mo-ah. Cars will run-over
Dogs and cats, birds, squirrels, butterflies,
Ants—and other cars and people. Cars will
Run-over-Jesus, Mohammed, Buddha, Zoroaster—
Abraham and Moses. I mean—cars will
Run-over-you in Baltomo. Cars will
Run-over-Mother Mary, Queen Mary,
Your Mary, My Mary and Sister Sadie.
I mean—cars will run-over-you in B'Mo,
Man. Cars will run-over-Henry Lee, McAbee
He Hung Low and Tojo, I mean-
Cars will run-over-you in Balt-Mo.
Cars will run-over Nuns, Bishops,
French Chefs and Khruchev, I mean—
Cars will-run, right over you—they
Will run you down—and run-over-you
In Baltimore. Cars will run-over-Einstein
Frankenstein, Bach, Mozart and Alain Locke, Yeah!
Cars sho/will run over you in Bal-tee/mo;
And high on the fatality list are drunks,
Junkies, Cripples, white dogs, black dogs,
Chinese dogs, brown dogs, red dogs, cats,
(Whatever their color) and old folks. Cars
Will definitely run-over-you and yo/mamma,
My/mamma, and a whole lot of white folks.
Cars will hit yo ass
In charm city, Man. Cars will run
Over King Kong, Hop-along, Cassi-dy
and Mr. Bumblebee, Cars will run-over
You on the sidewalk, in the alley
On your steps—your parking lot/and on the Block
This shit's gotta stop/.

Uh-huh, yeah. But I mean—cars WILL
Run-over-you in Baltimore (unless, of course
You have a lucky charm in your pocket)
But guess what? They don't sell-em
In Bal-tee-More-a. And this suppose
To/be the Charm city!) Umph.

Saying Somp-in
4-26-96 - 12:22 p.m.

I see Yo/boy
Walk'n down the avenue
about half-past-three
in the 'morning
wid-his pants dropped down, down
near to his knees
at which time
I cut down ma speed
to about ten miles per
and yelled out my window
Hey!
Pull dem got/DAMN pants up,
and while I was speeding off
Yo/boy was reaching for his "Iron"
and cursing all at the same time:
"Muh-fuck-ER-R-R—
Come back and stand up like a man,
MAN!"

I Remember Baseball
April 14, 1996 - 9:50 a.m.

In my hometown
they would'nt even let us sit in the Bleachers
in Kafer Park
We sat way over on the side
parallel with homeplate and the catcher
in some broken-down benches
each stacked over top the other
especially built for colored folk.
And no matter how many balls we brought back
after they had been knocked over the fence
we still had to sit in our assigned places
You might have thought
that this would have discouraged us
perhaps even causing us to cheer
for the opposing team?
Instead we sat over there
and sometimes stood
and argued and fussed with the umpire
louder than the ones sittin' in the Bleachers.
And when the game was over
if the home team lost
we cried louder than the ones in the Bleachers
And if they won
we cheered and whooped and hollered
as though we could'nt wait for the next game
when we could sing,
"Oh Happy Day!"
again?

Civil War
12-15-94 - 3:40 a.m.

It was all about slavery and me—really;
Although they tried to put it on
Everything else BUT me and slavery.
But for real—fuck the causes of the war
they said was caused by:
>The insanity of leaders
>Territorial conflict
>Machiavellian principles
>The Missouri Compromise
>The election of Lincoln
>The beginnings of the Republican Party
>Capitalism

Fuck all that
>The war was about slavery—

About reducing human beings
>To inanimate objects

About turning God's Crown Princess
>Into Footstools.

The civil war
>Was the devil's gift

To the future hangups of
>Racism and new slavery

That's why we're going
>to D.C.,

You and me—
>"One million strong

Before long."

A Wheelchair Speaks
July 16, 1994 - 5:15 p.m.
(No ridicule intended, or mean spirited aspersions cast,
in the rendition of this poem. Its only purpose,
hopefully, is to raise the conscious level of those who
become disabled as a result of drugs, and the potential
disabled persons who continue to use either directly or
vicariously. Again, no abuse, embarrassment,
humiliation, or judgment intended against any
disabled person, however he or she became that way.)

I carry a lot of weight
around—a good deal of excess baggage
I don't need.

Some of it is guilt and devastation; but the most—
physical—material and real.

There are all kinds of reasons
why I'm here—shot gun blasts,
shot guns, car accidents, knife wounds
stabbings; but the biggest reasons
inclusive of all others
is drugs—more drugs and most of all drugs.
I get so damn tired of carrying
this dead/weight, paraplegic around,
but what else is there for me.

I got to keep on gett'n practice
cause these yo/boys keep on "pushing"
drugs—more drugs and most of all—drugs.
Ut-oh—hold/up—l just heard a shot!
 gotta call my wheelchair buddies
so they can get ready to wheel another
Yo/boy 'round the hood.
He deserves me though. He did everything
to get me.

Oh well—the parks filling up
with some more of my wheelchair comrades.

Will these Yo/boys ever learn?
They'd better! They're running
out of wheelchairs and handicap stickers.
Ha!

In the Street of New Orleans
April 16, 1978

Folks crowding/up
on each other
throwing pennies
in the circles
almost always missing that little Blk hat
so properly put in place
by Tap Dancers
just trying
to get a little
soul/money for
survival—
just trying to
get a little fun
out of this funky life—
just trying to say/what
their heart knows
by soul stomping
and soul strutting
on the street of Bourbon
in New Orleans
I wish that/ole drunk
would stop passing
the cup around
hell he can't dance, anyway
all he wants is some wine,
some fire
so he can turn/on,
too!

CHASING A DREAM LIKE DUNBAR

Paul dreamed
    Langston Hughes dreamed
        Martin Luther King dreamed
        Poets dream
I dream, too
    A lot
Always expecting
    great things to/do—
Perhaps crossing the Alps
Like Hannibal?
    Maybe to write a catchy song
Like Duke Ellington
Compose a delightful opera
    Like Scott Joplin, Tremonisha?
What about a brilliant Shakespearian actor
    Like Ira Alderidge
Perhaps even a great football player
    Like Jim Brown
    Maybe Buddy Young/or
To write like James Baldwin
    Is alright for some?
I know!
    Maybe a dancer
    Like/Bojangles?/Hey!
Let's conquer outer/space
    Harness the ocean's roar;
Jump on a star—
    Sit on a cloud
And glimpse the face of God;
Then ride to earth on a rainbow
    And find a cure for AIDS.
I dream of power,
    Power to acquire—
    Diamonds or pearls, or be

President of America, or
    King of the world!
Sometimes dreams come true,
    Paul's did.
He died a great man
    So did Langston
    So did Martin
    Maybe—????????
Yeah, I believe it now
    Dreams do come true
That's why
    I'll keep on chasing
My dream
    No matter how far it seems
Because dreams come true—
    Dunbar's did!

Africa Eternal
10-20-90 - 7:43 p.m.

I wanna always
    be reminded
    of the drum
Where life for/me
Begun, in the sun—
    of Afri/CA
As a star/
glowing, brilliantly
Through the scenarios
    of humanity
Ever sustaining
Its eternal place in history
And in the destiny
    of melanin people!

True Love

In an old country town
And in a very old
Country Church
People didn't get along
For all kinds of reasons—
You know,—the usual—
envy, jealousy, grudges,
resentment; Yes, and even color!
It was that kind of church;
It was that kind of town.
That winter—which- by the way
was the coldest ever—
A new minister came to town
His name was Dr. Feelgood.
And so that next Sunday
Was Quarterly Meeting Day
And Lottie—Dottie—
And everybody was there
dressed in their Sunday Best.
There was a big ole
Heater in the center of the church
where they held the preaching
and all.
And the minister got there
Before everybody else
And he built a flaming hot,
Red hot fire—
When the people
began coming in
they took their usual seats—
way-away from each other
AND the red hot heater
by this time
was flaming!

As the service progressed
And the hall got colder
And the heater hotter
The people began inching
toward the heater—
They kept on inching until
The room got colder
And the heater got hotter
until they began touching
each other.
In the meanwhile
the minister's text was:
"If I could just touch
the hem of His garment."
When Dr. Feelgood
announced his topic,
He immediately proclaimed
"A Love Feast"
This is when everybody
begins to touch one another
And kiss each other
and say kind words to one another.
Then a sister got up and sang, "Amazing Grace,"
After which a brother sang, "Look where God
done brought us."
And they all ended up singing one of the old
time favorites, "I'm climbing
higher mountains—trying to get home."
With that
Dr. Feelgood cleared his throat
and everybody got up singing—
"What a Fellowship"

And they held hands—
some shouting around that ole hot stove
as each brother and sister
knew in his heart that
this was the beginning of true love
in that ole church on the hill.
And before the service
was over people
had forgotten all about
themselves and began to think
about their neighbor's concerns.
This was the first
real service this ole church
ever had.
It was an experience
that they had never had
before—True Love!
They never forgot that day
nor the love they had shared, together
for the first time
in all their Christian endeavors in the past!

At the Turn of the Century
December 17, 1994 - 10:17 p.m.

I did'nt know
      God made Honky Tonk
Angels—
      And I don't-believe
God brought-me this far
      Just to leave me.
Out of slavery
      More than a generation
We figured we had it made
      In the shade
Ha! Then here come Simon Legree's son
      and all his sons and devils doing
some mo' shit. Yeah!
Like this was not the day God had made.
It was the Devil's holiday—time out
      For the beast,
Dressed in academic frocks
      Caps and gown and all
Running up and down the country side measuring
heads
      Black heads and fleshy butts
and putt'ng it all on me,
      But hold it/
The chimpanzee ain't got no butt at all
      What that make him—
A chip/munk?
Anyway—we held our heads up
Built institutions, kept the faith
and waited by the side of the road
For Marcus Garvey.—
      "Back to Africa, Ya'll!"

Sweet Spring
(To Mom & Pop)

Cardinals don't come out
'till spring
     (Wine taste better
     then too)
But that to me doesn't
mean a thing
     If sunshine and
     laughter don't
     come right after.

Roses bloom nicely in pretty
weather,
     (Dresses get shorter then
     too)
And life gets so much
better
When we welcome those
     days with their
     crazy ways!

Never saw a water-fall in snow
     (Bums don't sleep
     in parks either)
And some folks just don't like the show
     That nature puts-
     on for us to
     scorn.

Guess Leprechauns paint
the forests so,
     (Some people don't
     clean until spring.)

Don't see those pastel
colors though
      'Til Spring is come
      with dance and
      fun.

No wind for kites 'cept
springtime
      (Black boys want
      to fly planes
      now)
Kites fly swell when winter's
behind
      A toast to the hills
      with their
      daffodils.

Spring brings brooks, and lazy
meadows
      (Boat 'n fish'n
      's good too)
That rustic look and jolly fellows
      Ah, signs of
      Spring, nature's
      magic brings!

The Only Child, Me
4-19-91 - 12:46 p.m.

What happens
  When it's over/
  When
        The bell rings
And school lets out
And I'm left alone—
    Just my homework
    And me
To/carry home.
It's madness
    For "only children",
No sisters n' brothers
    To blame things-on
    No/body to worry,
        Nobody to/care
Wow.
        Sometime's school's a happy
place—
Cause in that
            space
I got company
    Friends to play games/on
Instead of playing
    with that ole pillow
I grew up with—
    Oh, it's no fun
        For anyone
To spend nights at home
With no friends to comfort
And to sleep alone.
But God's still there
He's family and friend—
He's company for me
On Him I depend.

SPRING

This special reason
again this season—
to write pretty phrases
with odes to the sages;
but the pleasure
we seem to treasure
is to recapture spring
and the joy it brings.

Life's on the wind
enjoy it then—
cardinal's singing
Yes, Spring is bringing
a golden morning
in life's fresh dawning.

Gaze upon the sun
Spring's already begun—
walk in the showers
gather April flowers
an experienced thumb
is lots of fun
Plant some green;
it'll soon be seen.

Catch the breeze
in nature's trees—
Touch the sky
The logic we'll deny.

Spring is on the moor
tis winter I deplore—
Another nature is ours
through all life's hours
I love you spring
You're my everything.

MY FATHER
GOSSIE MACK HUDSON
(Dedicated to my Daddy)

My Father is a special man
That God, Himself, picked out;
He's nice to be around, my Dad
Real nice to think about.

My Father has a clever way
Of being dear and sweet;
He's made my whole life
　　　just worthwhile
My love for him's complete.

He's always made me proud
　　　of him
so glad to be his son;
I'll always thank him
　　　for his help—
The good for me
　　　He's done!

THE ICE MAN COMETH
(Message to the Projects)
(This poem is sincerely dedicated to Little Ronald "Billy Boy" Hill, "Ba-Ba", and Andrea)
November 27, 1982 - 10:57 p.m.

So sad
when you see the Meat Man
back of a
PO-lice car
with red, flashing lights
in front of a seven/story/bldg
where people hidden
within their little dark apts
signifying and looking/down
in awe
at the Meat Wagon
and folks
standing round
on the playground
while Blue Coats and White Coats
bring the stone/cold/dead Brother
out of the bldg
then load it up
and speed away,
Whatever the age
of the fallen Brother
(36 they say)
he stands
for all of the fallen
Victims of Blk self/hate
who could have been Baldwins,
or perhaps Richard Drews,
maybe even Malcolm Xs
When will the killing stop/

when will Brothers and Sisters
learn that the only
Real Message
for the Black Community
is "Love Thy Brother
as you would yourself."

Ronald Wilson Reagan: Goodbye
11/11/94 - 2:25 p.m.

I understand that:
>Leprechaun acting
>Flag—waving
>Gospel stomping
>Cowboy gun tote'n
>Rifle shoot'n
>B-rated movie making
>Bubble-gum blowing
>Peanut-candy breaking
>Corny joke slurring
>Jellybean eating
>Conservative sharing Ronald Reagan

Is senile—now
What a LIE-I-I-I-I/
>He was already senile
>BEFORE he got in office.

Now that he's long-gone
SO LONG!
>But wait a minute/
What about all those negro, uncle tom—
pusillanimous, Lilliputian, yahoo
Colored folk who voted him in office?
Goodbye to them, too!

In Memory of an African/Roman Emperor, Septimius Severus
(For my students)
November 14, 1994 - 1:15 p.m.

Europeans from Herodutus and Thurcydides to
    Edward Gibbons and H.G. Wells;
    from Godfrey Higgins to Gerald Massey
    and from Winthrop Jordan
    to Anthony R. Birley
Have known about you, Severus;
    but they failed to document you, properly,
    out of ignorance—perhaps—
    or gullibility or both;
But now it's time—
Time for truth and consequences, time
    For uplift and light
    in the African American community.
2000 years ago Africans flew
Around the Heavens—built astronomical
observatories,
Smelted iron, painted the most marvelous
Pictures the world has ever known.
This appeared more than 2000 years before
The reign of a Black Emperor, like you, of the
grandest
Empire ever present in the history of the ancient
    world.
His name is/was Lucius Septimius Severus,
A prince—a Hannibal, buried
    in the red robe of glory
On AD, 21 1, and was
    placed in a vase—
    Prayed over and now:
That purple urn which holds his ashes—
That urn filled with the physical
remains of such a cosmopolitan Roman bureaucrat—
That urn running over with Roman imperial history—
    Is only the physical symbol of your body,

63

but it never held your spirit;
That African spirit eternal that lit
     up the ancient world with its pyramids
     and light houses and colossal statues;
That African spirit eternal behind
     the blessings
     In the messages
          of J, A. Rogers, and Jackson and Clarke,
          Of Asa Hilliard, Dungee and Van Sertima;
For it was not your blessed grand father—
     wealthy Roman Knight
     he was;
Nor was it your own genius
     Not even because of your
     phenomenal rise to power,
     nor the vigorous expansion
     of your imperial frontiers—
What made you, YOU was the eternal African spirit
     so much a part of all African peoples,
That same spirit which has been a catalyst,
     A sustainer
     A resiliency
Manifested in African, genius-like ability
To make "bricks without straw."
Clearly because of you and others like you
     that African spirit, so eternal—
     going back more than two million years—
The "brick", once rejected,
Is now the corner stone of the Temple.
Hail African Emperor—
     born April 11, 146 AD, Hail!
Hail African Roman Emperor—
     protector and army commander in Gaul, Hail!
Hail Imperial Emperor—
     governor of Galla, Pannoia and other
provinces, Hail!
Hail Caesar—HAIL!

One Million On Their Way
(For Marcus Garvey)
June 15, 1994 - 1:42 p.m.

Just you and me—One million strong;
Before long—Imagine.?
      African men, Black men.
      Colored men, Negro men
      Red men, yellow men—
      Brown men, mulatto men—
      Moes and Joes
One million strong, before long—
      Christian men and Muslim men
      Ignorant men and educated men
      atheist—agnostic
      Hip men—jive men
      Squares and Toms
      Conservatives and radicals
      Niggers and Negroes
      Low class—middle class—
      Ghetto men and elite Black men
      Seventh Day Adventist—Jehovah Witness
      Come-next-year, have no fear
We'll be long gone in the "Storm"
We'll be free and strong
      Before long.
We'll be coming
      by the thousands—ten thousands and millions
We're coming, Man we're coming—
      One million strong, before long.
"Sankofa bird, have you heard?"
Before long—look up and see
      We'll be in D. C.
      Just you and me—
One million strong, we're coming—
With those from the valley
And those from the top

We won't stop
Til we get there; Oh Yeah!
One million strong
Just you and me
In D. C., before long!

License Number VCR-299
9-20-90 - 4:03 a.m.

I parked
on the street
the other day
to enjoy my favorite
past/time activity—"writing poetry"
And out of no-where
came leaping Dan—the Man
guess who?
Neither skinheads nor klansman
Neither racist nor bigot—
It was a big-ole
fat/black
African American
poli/C/man
screaming: "Move Yo Car, Boy!"
Scared me half-to-death, (that damn fool)
but I got his license number though
and kept right/on writing
Ma poetry!

A Poem on the Battle of Antietam
Civil War, 1862

A few years ago, a visit to the historic Antietam Battlefield inspired me to write the poem below. Near the end of the experience, excitingly narrated by Dr. Jay Luvaas of the U. S. Army Military History Institute, Carlisle Barracks, Pennsylvania, Captain Ray Fender, U. S. Army Ordnance Corps, who invited my colleague, Dr. William Alexander, and me, remarked: "If that old Sycamore Tree there could only talk—the bullet holes are still in the trunk." As I looked over the Antietam Creek at the Burnside Bridge, and then glanced up at the old tree—standing on the edge of the Antietam Creek—I began to compose the poem.

Some research on the subject revealed that this tree is sometimes called button-ball or buttonwood tree. It belongs to the same genus as the European Plan Tree, Platamus Orientalis, The American Sycamore, Family is Platamus Ocadentalis, Linn.

Sources show that the common name of the tree has an interesting history. Ancient Egyptians named it "Pharaoh's Fig". Egyptians used the wood of this tree for their strong mummy cases. Its coarse grained wood is also used for furniture, boxes, woodenware, butchers' blocks handles, crates, etc.

Usually a big tree, 75 to 150 feet high, the Sycamore lives to an age of 500 or 600 years. It is the most massively effective tree in the Eastern United States.

Sycamores, whose limbs express strength, often stand on the verges of streams, leaning far out as if contemplating a plunge. The "Antietam Sycamore" must have been nearly 200 years old. Captain Fender said it was only a small, perhaps baby tree when the battle began on September 17, 1862.

Old Sycamore (Buttonwood)

Pharaoh's Fig Tree
In many places/
Maker-of Egyptian—
Mummy cases.
Grey-white limbs &
Red/brown branches
Touching the sky &
Taking your chances, but
What do you know/
Old Sycamoe'?

With heart/shaped leaves-,
Towering like stark
Cork-ridge twigs
& flaked-off bark—
You stand at the peak
Of the Antietam Creek, but
What do you know/
Old Sycamo'?

A young sapling then/
When it all began—
Growing very quickly
Amid the dust-,
Assaulted by birds—
Insects and brush
In summer heat
& winter sleet, but
What do you know/
Old Sycamo'?

What do you know/
Old Sycamo'—
On Sept. seventeen, a
Fearful day/

When 23 thousand/
Soldiers lay—
Dead, wounded & missing;
You always knew
That in '62
Your body still battered—
Bruised & blue, that
Twelve full hours
On the Antietam Way/That
Murderous day—
Of the entire war
Took place!

Confederates singing:
"My Mary-lan'"—
Crossing the Potomac
With Shell & gun
Where in ditches
They fought for ridges,
A battle for woodlots:
Cornfield & church, they
Were caught in the lurch—
Of a sunken—bloody lane;
The North won ground
But for miles around
The barns were filled
With their wounded.

Your roots seem to hide
The untold story
Of the Day, Men
Fought for glory.
But McClellan nor Lee
Saw the small baby tree
On the bottomland ridge
By the Burnside Bridge.

Near Harper's Ferry
& Hagerstown/Pike
The Battle began at Daybreak—
It lasted all day
& Lee would retreat
Yet South or North
Never claimed defeat!

You heard the cannon
Saw the shots that fell—
Lots in your bark
The trunk will tell, of
Sept. seventeen, that
Awful day—
At Antietam Creek
Down Sharpsburg way!

Over one-hundred/years
& you still recall—
That all—who fought
No matter what side, it
Was victory they longed for
& in honor they died—
  Yes you do know, Old Sycamoe'/
  Sycamore tree you know
  You know!

I Teach
May 1, 1978 - 1:20 a.m.

I teach the mind
that promotes productivity—
that transforms dreams into reality—
that emphasizes objectivity—
that demolishes prejudice—
that makes all men brothers
and all women sisters
For Brotherhood and Sisterhood/
I teach the mind through
creativity and imagination/
I teach the mind
that produces
the doctors and lawyers
the presidents and congressmen
the astronauts the entrepreneurs
the musicians and the prima donnas
the teachers and scholars
the administrators the bankers
the farmers the artisans the soldiers
the policemen the actors the models
the columnists the publishers
the authors the poets
the waiters the waitresses
the jewelers the collectors
the DuBoises the Shakespeares
the Freuds the Jungs
the trash collectors the taxpayers—
through dedication and commitment
God gave me the talent
to teach the mind—
ever so dramatically,
I Teach The Mind/

What's a Poem/or
What's In a Poem

August 3, 1978

What's in a poem—?
a pouring/out of the soul;
a way of saying "I love
    you"
when your pen lets you
    down
in a letter.

What's in a poem—?
a singing/out of the
    heart—
a release of your body
warmth
when you haven't quite
said/it in person,

What's in a poem—?
a tearful/heartful
    manifestation
of beauty
when your voice fails
to project "the real you"
through the telephone
    wires.

What's in a poem—? God!
all of the hope, feeling
ecstasy, fulfillment
optimism, faith
and satisfaction
welled-up in the soul
of a human body
that can send/out
envoys of Love and
    Beauty
in the various shades
and shapes of magic
    words

that if fortunate enough
to reach your hands and
    eyes
before I do
will bring
joy to my head
relief to my soul
and even Heaven
within my grasp!
That's what's in a poem!

JUST MAMA AND ME
May 21, 1990 - 5:05 p.m.

I see little boys
walking with their Mamas
And I remember
That Chinese Restaurant
We use-to go/to
And eat that Yat-Gaw-Mein with shrimp
And sip that tea
On Fulton Street
Then I remember that Christmas
In Brooklyn
When Mama told-me
There weren't no Santa/Claus,
And that play typewriter
I got
And then to look across the street
From my window
And see that Patsy's Mama
Bought her the same thing.
Oh such delightful days,
What a time we had—
Mama and me and the world.
I wouldn't have had it
Any-other-way
And I love her for/it!

On the Steps
11-4-93 - 8:45 p.m.

What kind of nonsense is this
bull shit
"When I came off the-steps. " What
In the hell do they be talk'n about
On the damn steps?" These Baltimoreans
Have the strangest way of expressing
Themselves! But I guess THEY know
What they be saying! Anyway—
I been thinking a whole lot
About that nonsensical phrase,
"On the steps." And I've come to realize
After all what they mean. They mean:
"When I did'nt know nut-ing."
Well—! Do they know anything
Now? I doubt it. They sho don't
Know how to stop killing each other
And they sho don't know nut-ing
bout stop using drugs? Do they?
So—so far as I'm concerned Balti
Moreans are still on the steps;
And I'll be damn glad when they
git off of-em!

Impressions
(To Florence Delories)

Valorous, Voluptuous African Woman
of a new world/
I kneel before Mt. Atlas
reverently hushed behind
the mortal veil
to pray/nay to beg
that you shall hold against
the world
> Your beauty
> and charm
to match the majesty of Mt. Kilimanjaro.
The cold shoulders of the sky
reach out for your warmth
> Black
> Woman

For you are
the sweet salt
and heat of the earth/
The Gods made your
bosom out of sunshine and flowers,
out of Neptune's Nectar—
tempting, appetitive—
strong like the wind
that shakes the corn/
Comely woman, Nilotic woman.
Amorous Woman. Watusi Woman.
> Pretty Eyed Woman!

Would that I lay
close on your body
to soak up
         Your love
         and
         your strength
through all eternity—
Yea, e'en through
Poseidon's watery shadows/
Perhaps, your own sanity and
warmth and
goodness and
     innocence and
        toleration
may protect a fool like me
who once tried to conquer—rather than love
        a
        sensitive
        heart like yours?

A "Warrior" Named Mandela
(Written for my friend, Amy)
July 15, 1993 - 6:57 p.m.

I dreamed
    I spent 27 yrs in prison
        In South Africa
Unjustly.
Then I thought about unity—
    Unity and solidarity
    Unity and apartheid
    Unity and the diaspora
    Unity and struggle.
    Unity means—NELSON MANDELA
But Mandela is African!
I've never been to Africa—
Never been in the bush
Or knew, first-hand;
What it's like hustling
Peanuts and bananas
On the slopes of Kilimanjaro.
Lake Victoria depicts royal splendor
So they tell me. I don't know?
I once taught a chap from the Cameroon.
He talked about the Sahara and the Savanna—
Gee, it would be swell
To see the desert
Where once stood Timbuktu,
Or visit, God forbid,
The old, ancient decayed slave pens

On the West Coast
And see ships sailing
Up and down the East Coast.
I've never seen a "real" warrior
                    Either;
that is, not in the flesh
If I had—
                    I wish it would have been/Mandela,
Mandela is a "Warrior".
You say, "Freedom Fighter",
I say
        WARRIOR!
That word means a/lot
                    To-me.
Mandela IS a "Warrior"—
A tall, velvet, Black
Stately, African "Warrior"-,
And I love even his name.
He's a warrior in his love
        For humanity, Blacks in the world
He's a warrior in his walking
        And talking in the African way
His presence and demeanor remind me:
        "He IS a Warrior
My warrior
        Mandela—
MY MAN!"

No Ordinary Man, Uncle Wilson
April 2,1994 - 11:10 a.m.

An original poem in memoriam of
An almost forgotten human being

I kinda of knew that just before his
Death he had prayed hard for grace and
forgiveness, because nobody was going
To come by. He knew that! God knows,
He had turned folks around from his
Door often enough, and kept the
Curtain pulled down so no one would
Dare knock at his door unless they
Were crazy or something. And yet with
All his reservations about strong
Drinks he was still arrogant enough and
Proud enough to have a conscience, and
Be concerned about what others thought
About him—you see—unlike some
Alcoholics, he claimed not to drink at
All; and he was very hostile and obstinate
About it! How could he let people come
In—in a house full of debris and
Filth and trash and garbage and leaky
Roofs and hole-ly floors, and ceilings
Propped up by sticks, and tubs catching
Rainwater and snow and whatever else
Fell from the high heavens—and wine
Bottles and whiskey bottles and cans and
Soda bottles and jugs and spit-tums
Full of snuff juice and remnants of

Chewed up and chewed down tobacco
Plugs and what all? How could he let
Somebody in there" How could he let anybody
In there? Yet this was no ordinary man-,
He may have been too lazy to take
A bath and turn his heat on so that
He wore several pants and shirts and
Underwear and socks on a daily basis,
Indeed, maybe he might have been
"bumy" but not a bum—a brilliant
Christian gentleman—a meticulous record
Keeper who dated everything, who almost
Taught himself entirely to read and to
Write—a man who became knowledgeable
Enough to pass the North Carolina
State board of examiners and become an
Outstanding insurance agent in Oxford;
A man who was conversant with well
Educated people on the contemporary
Issues of the day—a man whose mind
Dwelt on an analysis of Biblical quotations
And philosophical interpretations with a
Spice—well laid with common
Whimsical language and homespun,
Witty remarks—so reminiscent of an
Eric Hofler and a Will Rogers. No sir
Uncle Wilson was no ordinary man.
And even as the inebriated, wine
Addicted, alcoholic sot he became, he
Still managed to keep an abundance
Of food in his refrigerator and

Freezers, new books on the table, his
Lights and telephone on; and he apparently
Paid his bills on time—sometimes even
Before they were due. He was no ordinary
Man—perhaps irresponsible, certainly
Maladjusted and frustrated; but no
Ordinary man. They
Found him in the house—his late
Wife, Mrs. Florence P. Wilson had kept
So immaculate and dignified—and
In that God/awful room on top
Of all those sheets and blankets and
Pillows and debris—more like a
Funeral pyre than anything else—with
Both feet on the floor, his arms folded
Upward, his mouth open, and eyes fixed
On top of the ceilings, he had
Probably been praying—although he
Had given up—that his Maker would
Somehow forgive him. But he had
The unique privilege of knowing, that
At least while he lived, nobody
Could point the accusing finger at
Him—leastwise not to his face—
And he could go out peacefully,
Arrogantly, independently and religiously,
For he was no ordinary man, Mr. Wilson, and
In a certain, peculiar way—God
Had seen to it that he did not
Leave this earth in an ordinary manner.

Parents of the Ones Who Made It to the Top!
7-8-93 - 12:25 noon

We were the ones standing in the
Shadows before you did it! We
were the ones kneeling in the closets
And on the subways and trolleys
until our knees were skint and our tear
Stained faces were red as hot peppers.
We were the ones who stooped and bowed
And said and did whatever was
Necessary in order that no
Hurt, harm or danger or embarrassment
Befell you. We were the ones who
Always believed when nobody else did
We were the ones who kept the
Faith even when there was no faith
We were the ones who defended you
When nobody else would. We were the
Ones who lied, manipulated—anything
As long as you made it—We did'nt
Care. We only wanted you to be
Successful-SOMEBODY-no matter what.
And Now you're on top. Everywhere I
Go I hear your name and of your Fame.
All of this and you don't even
Stop to write us a single line that says:
"Dear Y'all, " or "Dear Mom or Dad,"
whatever? You don't call; you don't write,
and you seem to think everything's al/right
But it is'nt. You'll need us
Again—and guess what—WOW!
We'll come running
We'll like that! We know no
Other way. Let's face it—
We're PARENTS.
We can't do any better
And neither do we want to.

MY ETHIOPIA, MY QUEEN
(For my wife Florence)
6-26-90 - 8:35 a.m.

MY QUEEN/

    NONE MORE BEAUTIFUL

THAN YOU—

    ETHIOPIA

        MY WOMAN

DUSKY LADY

EMBODIMENT OF UNIVERSAL

        ILLS AND CURES;

YOU, WHOSE EYES

WET WITH TEARS/

AND EARS HEAVY WITH-OPPRESSION SHARED

BY ALL AFRICAN/MOTHERS.

    KEEP THE FAITH,

    COURAGE TO YOUR/SOUL;

BECAUSE OF-ALL EARTH'S QUEENS

THERE IS NO BRAVER—

      NONE GREATER

      NONE SO/BEAUTIFUL

        AS

          YOU!

MY GOD

(A Poem for Easter)
April 7, 1990 - 11:59 p.m.
Dedicated to my son,
Gossie Harold Hudson, Jr.

My God's hand print

Comforts my/soul, always.

In times of trouble when

I'm at the mercy

Of my adversaries

I follow my/God.

I do not see Him

But I feel His presence

So I look up/and

I behold Him—

Then I rise

And He leads me.

The Drummer
(Dedicated to Mr. Andre Drapper)
September 6, 1993 - 9:45 a.m.
Written at Payne Memorial African Methodist
Episcopal Church, Labor Day, During a Preparation for
a City-wide Revival at Pier Six.

Amid prayers and religious discourses
an old/time country sermon
choral singing and introductions;
among Big Shots and Grassroots People
    And the shrills and thrills
of a happy congregation;
among the jubilant clamor
    of the tambourine
between jazzy trumpet licks
and the jingling vibrato
    of the organ
I heard the drummer—
stretching his magical sticks
over the membrane of a hollow frame.
    The guitar was majestic
    so was the trumpet
but it was that drummer!
Balls of sweat running down
his silky black face
on to his hands
where gripped 2 sticks rising up
    going down and all around—
boy—did he beat
        those drums
that morning!

It was church music, though
like the rushing of a mighty wind.
    The drums made ma feet light—

like I was tiptoeing down Broadway.
It was a moving experience,

                up/beat
Embellished by a lot of hand clapping
                disco-beats
and Amens and uh-huhs
and wows and yeahs.
A good drummer can make you
Wanna go places and do things—
skiing down Kilimanjaro,
jumping rope on the moon
or swimming up the Mississippi River.
Gee, I wanted to just fly—
do somersaults on Mars
catch a falling star—even.
I ended up wanting to clap my hands
and I did, rather rhythmically—
especially during the crescendos,
                and dramatic pauses;
only a professional could drum like that
Only a gifted musician could be that superb.
That brother sho kicked that bass
And smacked those cymbals. He did it
until his entire drumset rang-out
                Hallelujah
                Hosanna
        To the King of Glory!
But it wasn't just beating

                The drums—or
kicking the bass
that got next to/me,
it was that steady beat, too—
        rhythmic and captivating
        impressive and exhilarating—
making all who listened
want to dance
jump up and down and shout—it
even made my heart flutter
        a little bit

Cause I still remembered playing
with Grady Tate with my own "Sax"—-
when ("Nard", as we called him then)
use to call that kind of drum beating
"blowing up a storm,"
God! You wouldn't have known.
It was a church! It was more
like a jam session, but it wasn't,
It was the revelation of the "Holy Spirit"
And I enjoyed every minute of-it—
because my feet just
        couldn't keep still.
My hands seemed to clap
        right-by-themselves.
Ah-h man, that long-leg
skinny, clean-head, tall, lean,
lanky Black Brother
could sho/nuff kick them drums
                man.
He was bad-d-d-d-d-d.
He made my heart sing!
Thought I'd never stop stomping
'N pattin' my-feet.
I damn/near started
        Ta get my little "SAX"
        And blow a little taste
                Myself
Sure was a beautiful way
to begin a Labor Day
                Morning.
My heart sang
        all the way home—
still remembering THAT drummer,
One of the best I've ever heard!

REVOLUTION!
June 18, 1995

No time for meetings
No time for speeches
No time for writing
No time for Uncle Thomas
No time for Aunt Jemima
No time for toming
No time for jiving
No more preaching,
It's time for REVOLUTION/folks.
   Time to git/down Brother/man
Let's move on down the line
It's REVOLUTION TIME, man
   "Moses saw the rainbow sign—
   No-more-water, Jack
   The FIRE Next TIME!

Remembering Happy Times
(To Gertha)

Sometimes—
I remember
those wonderful years
when we were young
and gay
sitting in those classes
in elementary school
wishing the bell would ring
so we could get out
and jump and play
and fall/down and throw
snow all over each other
while the old principal/sage
with his arms folded neatly
behind him
would stare at us,
perhaps even wishing
he could fall/down too
and fill up his shoes with snow;
then the bell would ring
and I'd hit you
with a snowball
and dash inside
only to stare out
of the window and
dream of what fun
we were going to have
throwing some more snow
when school let/out
and when I would go/back home
to my little community
of Poor, but Proud Black Folks
and help Mommy
to help me be Somebody!

High On Coffee
(For Recovering Addicts Only)
July 15, 1990 - 12:13 a.m.

Room filled with people
    all colors who drink coffee
Knowledge and freedom to help
live life on life's terms.
    People/folks
        More than bad
Got up and shared—
their story, a life of dignity/
Honesty and truth.
    I was impressed!
Some shared on love, some unity
Some cried. A silence ensued?
Because somebody else carried a message—
Not of hope,
    but a D.O.A.
Caused by dope
He/would chair the meeting
    on Monday,
And now I—
        Feeling "high"/
Got/me some mo
    of that coffee.
I had my way
I got "high" on N. A.;
Coffee opened/up my mind
In time/
        I went home
to delight in a new knowledge—
A new world
        And a new talk!

COMMENCEMENT AT A BLACK UNIVERSITY:
IT WAS THE DREAM...
5/23/1993 - 4:30 p.m.
This poem is dedicated to my president, a man of
respect and honor: Dr. Earl Richardson,
President of Morgan State University

They marched—
Walked with marshalls
And Chiefs and Queens and Kings
Behind the Scepter
Toward their Black President
And the band played-on.
The African drum/beat filled the air
As they marched
To the cadences of the War March
Of the Priests (Some already dressed
In African garb)
They're graduates, now—
With bachelors and masters and
Doctorates in their heads and feet
(Some already in the military).
Oh, how they DID march-with
Grace and poise and dignity.
Commencement, Yes commencement
In all its rega-li-ty
Pomp, circumstance
And ma-jes-ty.
Yet/underneath its arrogance
Awesome astuteness
And exuberance,
Beneath it all, the dream—
See how it, gleams
For they'd passed the test
And now: "Success for the Best."

The Dream sustained us
       From Af/ri-CA
       To Ame/ri-CA
The Dream brought us
Through the "Middle Passage"
       And the Simon Legrees
       And the Bilbos and the Ms. Anns;
But we had Langston and Martin, and Kennedy, too
And so we held on to the liberation dreams
       Of our forebears
And they kept us, sustained us;
Sometimes we forget the "Dream"—
That jet-Black,
       Strappling Black
       Dream that elevated us—
       Enlightened us;
But we must always remember
"The Dream" symbol—
Because the Dream mirrors our African
Roots, so necessary
       In the destruction of anything
Detrimental to our advancement
       As a people,
       An African people/
The DREAM continues...

THE ORGAN PLAYER
Good Friday, April 9, 1993 - 12:00 noon

There is something delightfully impressive about the organ
  player when
He sits way above the pulpit by himself expressing those
  melodious
Concertos and symphonies dating back to classical times
  when a musician
Or any other artist like a Leonardo Da Vinci or a Schiller
  was a king.
Such grace and poise and pomp ringing from that organ,
  and there he sits—
Perhaps looking a little lonely, but he really isn't because
  he's right at home
With his instrument sounding soulful music streaming from
  its pipes.
Here and there I can even hear the organ bells ping and
  that delights my soul even
More with their poignant notes which lift my spirits to a
  mountain
Of joy and peace. Then comes the singers. Just then the
  pastor
Breaks through the beauty of it all by calling the church to
  order. Instinctively
The choir sings. In the meanwhile, everything is spoiled.
  The atmosphere
Grows sour, and in that brief moment, the organ player
  returns quickly to the
Valley where he plays the organ for us mere mortals of
  mediocrity,
PITY!

WISDOM
Dedicated to the late Maggie McCall
and all of her children)

WISDOM,
is someone from life's high mountains
who knows that Black Healing
comes from time and space sliced/up
by-knowledge tunneled deep in History
where answers to worldly complexities lay.
WISDOM,
is Black Griot from A-ke-bu-tan, ai-yi-yi-yi-yi!
Afri-KA, a whirl of forever
circles of Heritage moving eternally
Propelled by wisdom, kept intact
by Griots—you, Mama Maggie.
WISDOM,
is Lucy, First Lady of Afrika
Australopithecus, 3.75 million yrs. old
coming-up from Homo-habilis, erectus, sapien
From the Golden Age of Timbuktu to Black/Negro
Slavery to " Freedom" to S. C., to N. Y.
WISDOM,
is Family-building tradition—
Kwanzaa: Harambee, Uhuru-Uhuru Kumba-Nia
Mahoganied experiences
for community development
necessary for Liberation!
WISDOM,
is knowledge for counseling—
Goods to share
Help to give
Love to spread/And
a God to glorify!
WISDOM.

What If
October 7, 1993 - 8:55 a.m.

What if all the people not on drugs
    or selling drugs
    decided to see to it
    that no drugs—or drug deals—
    or selling drugs did not occur
    in their space—at home
    on the job, church, mosque,
    wherever? What If?
What then if all the drug pushers
    had to sell drugs at home
    and in their own space.
    What If?
What if African American
    communities set up a moratorium
    on all drug connected killing?
    What If?
What if they/decided
    that for the next sixty days
    there would be no more killings
    in the Black community?
    What If?
What if—if a killing, murder,
    shooting, whatever—did occur,
    the "hood" (neighborhood), would take care of it.
All by themselves with no police.
What if?

A Smile For Freddie
7-15-1994 - 11:55 p.m.

I set
her up
I had
to I
knew how
she felt
about me
but my
brother sitt'n
there in
that wheelchair
paralyzed needed
an orgasm
and she
was just
the right
person, So
I disregarded
my own
desires and
went ahead
with it!
It was

worth it
all when
I saw
that happy
smile on
my brother's
face. Anyway—
my chance
will come
later. In
the meanwhile
my brother
feels-good
looks-good
laughs excessively
all the
time—wow!
Perhaps my
time will
come tomorrow
or never!
Who knows?

RIGHT ON, HOMEBOYS!
5-17-94 - 10:30 a.m.

Some say it. Is it true?
Were the Jews, Slave Traders?
    If they were not
Let's bring sanctions
    Against the perpetrators
Of the lie,
    If they were
Let's just scream:
    "Right on, Homeboys!"
Some say it. Is it true?
Was the Jewish Holocaust
    Worse than the African Holocaust?
If it were
    Let's bring sanctions
Against the perpetrators
    Of the Lie,
If it were
    Let's just scream:
"Right on Homeboys!"
Some say it. Is it true?
Others—Jews, Native Americans, Japanese—
    Have received reparations
But African Americans have not
    But Should?
If this is untrue
    Let's bring sanctions

Against the perpetrators
        Of the Lies.
If the statement is true
        Let's get some homeboys
TOGETHER—
        And make somebody pay
And then scream:
        "Right on HOMEBOYS!"

A Dog Named Cha Cha (Windy)
(In the emergency hospital room
in New Orleans)

He was brown and fuzzy
and Chinese looking
for a bone / a blk
bone. And I in
sudden feelings
of superior-ity
was no author-ity
on dogism—
Cha Cha-ism/
never thought
he would bite me
not bad me / didn't
I have the scars
to show from recent
dog warfare that
he/though
ferocious
looking was no
match, for me? / But
He was:
I should a had
better sense than
to try to
stare that dog down/
he sho/showed me/

There I was propped/up
on his chair—
the place where He lay—
Smoking cigarettes
and blowing smoke
In His face
and on His head
And patting my lap
For Him to jump / up on.
I was so busy talking
and jiving
that I didn't see his eyes
those mean / dog—eyes
when I said:
"I ain't afraid
Of him
I'll cut some sense in
    Him."
He sho/showed me—
you betcha He sho/showed
    me
Right On Dog
Or Cha Cha
or windy
Or whatever they call you.
What made Him mean
was that rub

in his hair
messing it all up
"I gon getcha
He barked."
Then he jumped
right in my chest—
in my hand
trying to git to my throat
That ole mean
dog.
When he bit
into my skin, my
blk/skin, and the blood
flew out and the guts
hung out, I knew
then that wud'nt
no dog
but a Frankenstein, a wolfman
bent on my destruction/
my skin Destruction/
my HAND DESTRUCTION/
"Oh Lordy me
If I ever be
in the vi-cin-ity
of a dog named Cha Cha—
may I turn to a Man-Man
and BITE Him Back!

Make Life!
September 17, 1993 - 9:51 a.m.

"Man," you're smart
> And you know everything—

You can make a circus
> Or a fairground swing/

Now since you're so smart
> And you know what to do

I wonder about "life"
> Can you make that too?

You can make the chemicals
> To make you high...

You can make the
> Voices come through the sky

You can make the
> Cars go to and fro

You can even make
> T.V. and radio;

But try real hard
> And see if you can—

Make me a heart
> and then make a man?

Barnum and Bai-ley

No need to lie
I DID know about Barnum and Bailey
When I was growing up
But we never went to it
It cost too much money, man
And besides that's where
The white folks hung out.
Where we went, was to the carnival
Where we could "dig" the side show
And the jig bands
And those pretty little brown girls
Kicking up their heels and stuff
And me wishing I could blow my sax
With the band (sometimes I did.)
Yeah!
It was the carnival and the minstrel show
That pumped me up; and all that jazz, like—
"Love don't mean a thang
If it ain't got that swang"
That's what says it for me, even today
You see—not Barnum and Bai-ley.

Nostalgia
7-28-94 - 9:58 p.m.

It does not seem likely
That these eyes of mine will ever
be filled the majesty
Of old Cape Cod
      Or the bazaars of Baghdad
      Or a night in Tanzania.
And as for the Pyramids along the Nile
They're for lovers only—anyway.
And although I've been to Coney
—even ate Tootsie Rolls for two;—
I've never seen ole Delancy Street
They sing about. I passed through
Paris so fast, I forgot all about
The Eiffel Tower ... And, gee! It
Seems like I've spent a whole life time
Trying to find those Mending Walls
Robert Frost painted so beautifully,
And wrote so convincingly about
In his poems.
By the way? I wonder if it's really
Possible to go around the world.
In eighty days, or fly to the moon;
Or sit on top of ole Smokey?
I wrote a poem about Kilimanjaro
But—there's no use kidding myself—
I know I'll never see the snow-OR
The mountain.
They say you can sail around
On the inside of Vienna? I don't know?
But it sounds like fun,
Maybe I'll finally get to Africa
      Or the Caribbean one day;

I blew my chances when the Black Hebrews
Asked me. Wow! Biggest mistake I ever made
In my life. Oh well—
Like they say: opportunity knocks but once,
But why am I never at home?
Anyhow—my aspirations are higher
Now-a-days. Jack, I'd like to go
         To Mars or Jupiter-Venus
Just travel in outer-space
Until I get tired. This poem is gett'n
Real crazy. I haven't even discovered
America, yet. I mean I've never ever
Been to Disneyland or Arizona
For that matter. But so what,
I dream about it all. As a matter of fact
I travel in outer space often—almost
Every night. That's how I get to sleep
Yes, I dream a lot—and however
I end up—if I ain't high
Did'nt kill anybody
I figure I've had a pretty successful
Life. Whatever? I feel mighty good
Right now. And what ever I have not
Accomplished, I've accomplished it
Anyway—cause I say I have
And that's the real conquest
Is'nt it—Self Esteem (You know,
Feeling Good About Myself!)

MEDIOCRITY
1-9-91 - 11:10 p.m.

I don't know why
       I continue to write!
No/body, I mean
       but no - o - o - o body
seems to read anything
       I write—
mainly cause I don't show it
       to anybody.
Maybe I'm scared
       I don't know
or perhaps
       I realize
That I'm no writer anyway
Least of all a poet;
Yet I do feel
       The need to say—something/only
I wonder just what?
I wish I could describe
       Those Saturday's in New Bern
"Five Points," that is,
       When I wuz growing-up
When George Downing's wife
       Served the best home/cooked meal
         in town;
When club or joint Zanzibar
       was jumping like mad.
When the Minstrel came to town
and performed on Kilmonick Street,
       where everybody sold liquor,
Stump-hole (White Lightening) at that,
Except that Beauty Parlor
My mama used to work-in (Alfreda's)
Boy! I bet that'd make
       for some pretty good poetry/

Maybe even a novel or something
        If I could figure it out?
And, wow—those free Medicine Shows
        Where comedians and musicians
In the field behind Barber-row (alley) performed
Or that guy who whistled
        With his lips closed
In Five Points by that shoe shine parlor I worked in
        or that hustler who beat/me out of my last
                money
With that "Three-Card-Molly" trick.
Gee I wish I could describe
        That harmonica player—
His favorite tune was Collard-Greens.
        As he'd slip that harmonica
        over his teeth
                blew it with his nose
He'd clap his knees
        With the same harmonica
Never losing a beat.
Yes, I wish I did have the creativity
        of a James Baldwin
or the subtlety
        of an Ameer Baraka
or the dignity
        of a Margaret Walker
if I did
        I'd put that poem
                Together
I'd write that classic novel, too
And Gossie's name would last
        For an eternity
                Maybe!
But it'll never get done
        Not because I don't want-to

But because I lack
      The creative know/how
So I guess that whatever I do
      Whatever I write
Will just have to-be-for
      This moment only—
      The true historian I am,
      A fitting memorial
      To mediocrity
Because the poet writes
      For an eternity

Sisters in the Marketplace

We come together
In the Same space
To ask HIS blessing;
But, mainly because we know
That when more than one
Gathers in the marketplace
We draw strength
From each other
And from the Centerfold: God.
Sometimes we meet in the marketplace, mentally
Because prayer is boundless
And God's miracles, matchless;
Therefore, when we think, Under the inspiration of
    God,—
We are there, anywhere
And everywhere. We're like that
Us sisters—all of us concerned ones
Who live by spiritual principles!
Our name is Legion.

For we are many.
Because many stand with us
In spirit and in love and in doing!
We're the visible mortar
    In the marketplace
That holds the stones
    In place
While we stand
    In the Potter's house
Molding a wheel of love
    For our sisters
Who are on dope; sisters
Who are victims of child abuse, sisters
Who live in penal institutions, and sisters
Who have lost faith and hope
    Of ever moving

Beyond their devastation
In life's tragic circumstances.
        We are the visible ones
In the marketplace
With the iron fists in the velvet gloves
        Who tend to the sick
        Give service to the needy, and
        Give solace to the faint of heart.
We are the sensitive ones
We are the spiritual ones
We are the comely ones
We are the children of God, and
We are legion—many
We are creators, developers, overcomers,
We make the world
        We ARE the world.
Come to the market places
And see our faces!

Reality
8-26-1994 - 6:40 p.m.

Neck, arms, chest, ankles, fingers
Surrounded with expensive silver and gold
Red, Black, and Green baseball caps turned
sideways—
Half/a shirttail out; pants dropping
Down—almost to his knees
Mouth wide-open chewing gum
Like "nobody's business"
Singing: "Git yer guns-out"
While at the same time slapping/hands
With somebody who looks just like he
Does. Both will be dead, in jail, or shot
In the next two years!

Tribute to Minister Louis Farrakhan
(For Mr. Ralph Gilliam)
July 18, 1992 - 12:45 a.m.

Whatever coat of arms they wore, or

Badge of melanin covering their

Faces, all have tasted the bitter

Cup of slavery. But for the African

Hue—"enslavement", instead of "slavery",

Was more devastating and debilitating

Than for others. Some of these folk

Were broken by Simon Legree's lash

And whipped into submission.

Others—struggled, rolled

With the punches, and survived in spite

Of? Yet another, "stood fast"—looked past

The misery and chains of the moment and saw a ray

Of hope. These walked upright into the

"EYE of the storm" and created

The Nat Turners of their time and

Inspired the Louis Farrakhans of ours.

White Over Black

Can you hear the Tom/Drum
                    Beating of my mind—
Uh-huh.
Say man, can you hear the Tom/Drum
                    Beating of my mind—
Uh-huh,
Can you feel the sanity
                    In my mind—
Umph.
                    It's a white thing ya'll.
I mean—
It's a white thing, man, and
                    By the way
It's not about O.J. He really doesn't matter
It's a white thing, man;
                    Dunbar wrote about it
In Mr. "Cornelius Johnson", Ameer Baraka,
                    "The Dutchman"
And Baldwin and Douglass and Bethune
And Mary Church Terrell and William Wells Brown
And so many other writers
                    Who knew the pain
Of being Black in a white man's land
                    I mean—
It's a white thing, man.
                    It's about O.J.
Being with that blond, blue-eyed chick
                    And all those other white girls
It's a white thing man
                    And it just may be
That they gon look
                    At O.J.'s past
And hang his Black/un-huh!
                    It's a white thing, ya'll
It's about being Black
                    In a white man's land
It's a white thing, man,
Umph!

Storm's Coming
3-14-96 - 4:50 p.m.

However I prepare
for the vicissitudes of life—
triumphs and tragedies—it is also important
that I recognize with surest indication
of life itself—the dark side, too.
And yet—in that truth
I recognize more than ever now
that there's a better day coming;
and no matter what the storm
just before dawn
the light will come
for everyone.
>Yes—at the end of the dawning
>Comes the morning
It'll be alright
'Cause the storm's gone
And the sun has come
And we carry on
With a New Day begun.

Reflections At a Faculty Meeting, Arts and Sciences
10:20 p.m. - 8-20-91

I'm real glad
    That I connect with the "spirit"
Above the muck and mire
    Of mediocrity
Perhaps I'll never be/
    That scholar
    Or that renown scholar
They make so-much about/
    Like a/Quarles or a/Franklin;
But at least I don't have others
    To define me
Because I know
    What kind of scholar I am
And the service I give
    To others and to the community.
No, I don't need to be honored
    Or feted
    Or lionized
For being a great person—
I should never receive merit badges
For doing what God
    Sent me to be—
A friend of man, my people;
    And a teacher for our young minds.
(Old ones, too).

Crabs and B-Mo
(To My Buddy "Ms T")
7/1/92 - 12:43 Noon

You know—
I ought to REALLY love crabs! Being from New Bern
North Carolina, a peninsula
Maybe I'm expected to? I still remember
Going crabbing. Stopping by the fish market
And begging for fish heads. Then
Either renting a boat for 75¢. Or
Going on the James City bridge or crabbing
From the "side" of East-front-street,
It was a lot of fun crabbing
In shallow water where ya could
See the crab and he could see you. Then
Watching him grab that fish head
With his claws and me pulling
The fish head up along with the crab. —
(It was very easy because crabs are dumb)
Finally, the crab is just where
You want him, almost emerged.
Quickly you scoop the dumb crab
By topping his entire body
Claws and all, while
At the same time you flip him
Over, throw him in the sack
And amazingly he struggles
In vain to get away (after he's already in the toe sack)?
Oh how I loved crabbing
Until I came to B-Mo!
Here's what everybody
Should know before coming
To Baltimore?
When the temperature falls
50 below/in Baltimore, It's time
To go/to the waterfront

For some Crabs. But they'll get crabs
For any reason in Baltimore? If it's a-holiday.
Buy some Crabs If it's Mother's Day or Easter Sunday
Buy some crabs-, if it's Xmas Eve or Xmas Day
or a football game, baseball
or basketball game, boxing match
or just a picnic in the park—
then buy a WHOLE—lot of/crabs!
If the temperature goes up—
50 high; Or there 're clouds in the sky
Buy some Crabs. If relatives come
Buy some Crabs.
If you have a "cook-out", get some Crabs
If it rains, get some Crabs
If the sun shines, get some Crabs.
      Crabs go with fish
      Crabs go with oysters
      Crabs go with the weather
      Crabs go with crabs
      And crabs go fast
Around a Baltimorean.
If everything else fails, make
Some Crab Cakes, delicious Cream of Crab broth
      Soup of craps
      Fried crabs
      Boiled crabs
      Stewed crabs
      Baked crabs
      Crab salad
      Crab shala
      Just Crabs—
Especially if you live around Baltimore City,
I'm so damn sick of crabs
Oops! A Baltimorean's listening!

A Mother's Love

I don't know why
They always be hounding my son
My son says they lie on him
                    a lot.
I wonder why? He's such a darling.
He always tells me the truth.
He done made me aware
of all these policemen
School Teachers
                    And nosy neighbors
Just what the score is.
God! Why don't they leave him
                        alone.
My son never gives ME
                any trouble.
He has a good excuse
                for everything
But they keep on
putting burglaries and rapes
and things like that on him
                        anyhow.
Somebody's gon pay for this
Cause my son's alright
I love him, why don't others?
                        Oh well/
Somebody got shot
in a stick/up, and
They arrested my boy, last night,

but he didn/t do/it'
I raised him better n, that—
he don do dem things/.

They done electrocuted my boy
Yesterday—For Nothing,
What a shame—My Son).
I know he's in Heaven
Cause he was always
such an angel round the house.
Besides—he ain't never
done nothing wrong.
They been hounding him
All his life—
My Son wuz a good Boy/.

Reconstruction, 1865 to 1995
12-15-94/2:12 p.m.

I felt it; I knew it, I was free, at last
Thank God Almighty!
And so they made me a congressman
And then expected me to do
What they had tried to do
And failed;
But I fooled them
And learned what they forgot
And built institutions and organizations
And Universities and societies
And achieved miracles
They thought were impossible
And then set my sails for new worlds to conquer—
As I followed the Sankofa Bird
        Into real freedom,
Freedom of myself.

Ode to Queen Nzinga of the 17th Century
A Poem especially written for Kwanzaa, 1995-96
and for Sister Nzinga, Host of Just You and Me Radio
Programming, WEAA FM, 88.9
12-27-1995 - 11:45 a.m.

You!
Serving your own God, Tem-Bon-Dumba
Great Queen, generously Valiant—stubborn resister
cunning, prudent virago from the Mbundu nation.
Brilliant head of state and military leader
Astute agitator-propagandist
known as Ginga and Nzinga.
Sister of Fungi beheaded by the Portuguese;
Sister of Kinga Ngoli Bdondi
King of Ndongo (Angola)
And a member of the Jagas—
Human shield against Portuguese slave traders,—
Visionary—competent, self-sacrificing
        quintessence of early Mbundu resistance.
Creator of West Central African nationalism
called Monu-Kongo;
YOU, Sister Nzinga
Were recreated in Angola
On the West Coast of Akebulan
where sheep and cattle and goats
and horses and hogs breed,
And folks eat beans and sisal
and corn and sugar cane—
drink coffee and use tobacco for medicinal purposes.
Coming 'round to full circle
in your Royalty, 1623, age 41
You came to power a century ago—
ruling the state of Matamba
Until December 17, 1663.
You battled slave raiders for a generation
and negotiated a treaty with the Portuguese

in 1659—lasting until your death at 83.
We remember others, too
Who fought against enslavement
But mostly we remember YOU, Nzinga
Queen Nzinga, that is.
Thanks to the God of our fathers and mothers
You were reincarnated
And now, Queen Nzinga
You're back again, as SISTER NZINGA, (20th century)
to help us win, again!

Africa: One of a Kind
January 25,1995-6:45 a.m.

The beginning, the world
Where it all unfurled
Deep down in the womb,
in the conception of an amazing people—
A dark people, a pygmy people
A Watussi people, a slave folk
Who would heal the land, make the blind to see;
Who would heal nations and churches,
Make great contributions, discover
First and invent first and accomplish first
And make something out of nothing.
Africa immortal—one of a kind!

Bondage
May 12, 1989

Always
The rain masks me
and I feel real
        at last?
It's like a-blanket
To cover up-with
And allow me
To/do strange things
In secret.

I like to get-up
Underneath the rain
Cause I feel secure
But am I?

In the rain
I hide the "me", you/know,
        Cover up
All those deep/dark secrets
So I can do the things
I won't to
        In the Sunshine!
Come down rain
        Come down fast and hard—
I wish it would rain forever
Then I could always be me and do what I wanna;
But if I do
I'll "use!"

Winterend
(To Candy)

Some say fairies don't exist,
But I saw one in the park
yesterday.
Like magic she
painted the benches white
And made millions of tiny
needles to hang from
brush and foliage.
A flicker of her hand,
and a thousand mini snowballs
fell from Heaven.
Then she commanded the wind
and trees to sing,
And God's little four-legged
creatures watched in awe.
Just then, pecans, acorns,
and chestnuts emancipated
themselves.
And I saw an apple tree, and
a grapevine, and a patch
of strawberries;
Now the fowl could eat too.
But at noon the brightest star
came
And the good fairy left.
She'd only come to color winter you know,
And now under nature's brilliance
It was time
Time for a different canvas
And a new scene to sketch.

For Real, For Real
2-21-96 - 8:20

I went to a store
in a shopping center well known
for its foreign employees
from Mex-I-co, Jamaica, Korea
Deutschland, Iran, Syria and
Who generally just didn't give a damn,
about their customers, for real—
and that was the real deal—for real.
And, for real- for real?—
I got cowboy, boogaloo mad.
I politely asked the man,
Who spoke with a very incoherent
foreign dialect, "mister could you please tell me
where the handkerchiefs are?"
First he showed me some wooden Indians
then a toy hand grenade. And later
I got real American mad and asked
the man if he knew what 'n the hell
I was talking about, which he didn't!
But with the help of another buddy—employee
the man finally yelled out in a gravel
gripping, almost hypnotizing,
foreign accent, "OH YOU MEAN
HAND kerchiefs. This time I got real African
American, black-/Mad—
Imagine a foreigner—with-his-no-speaking, ugly/self
correcting my English my mother gave me!
That's a low/down dirty shame, man—
FOR REAL/for real.

A Brand New Way
11-19-1993 - 5:20 p.m.

Hey Man! Ya'll done
Really messed up this time;
And ya'll can be jiving
         And stifing
If n you want to
But the boogie—man's
        Sho gon catch
Ya'll this time—
And the man aint playing
          Either.
He done bought him some
        brand new horses
Some brand new squad cars
Some brand new shot guns
And hired some brand new niggers
To snitch on ya'll,
I mean ya'll gon stop
Killing my little brothers
         And sisters
No matter what it takes;
Wit ya'll lazy
       No-good-for-nothing
         Selves—
This shit gon stop,
      Man!

Santa Claus Assessment
Xmas, 1994
January 3, 1995

Yo/boy got tired of standing around
On the corner—at last! And besides
Somebody had stolen his comic books
And he didn't have nut-ing to read,
Yo/boy was in bad shape
Until "along came Jones" or "Jim Dandy
To the rescue" who gave Yo/boy
a new kind of literature—
Books by Ivan Van Sertima, John
Henrik Clarke, Anta Diop
Don't stop—Frances Cress Welsing
Drusilla Dungee, John Jackson,
A man of action—Yo/boy got Hip-hop
Mad! He did the "Tootsie Roll" first
Followed by the "Butterfly" and then
He said- "now listen, ya'll, Santa's
Got to go—Mo! With that
Yo kicked Santa down the chimney
His toy-bag, too; and then
The rest of the reindeer
And Rudolph flew.
Yes, Yo got baggie mad—
Kicked the xmas tree DOWN—
And began to clown. He
Tore down the stockings,
Smashed the toys—
Laid his knife on the rug
And broke down his mug
Yo got busy
Cause he was tired of Santa Claus,
So he got hep to his heritage
And turned over a new leaf,
And out of his relief

He said to himself, and everybody else—
This IS a new day
And I found me a brand new way—
No more Santa and reindeer
Nor Xmas tree for me,
No more jive
And Angels and toys from afar
Today it's Black Love
And Kwanzaa and Af/ri KA!

D/Cs Gone Funky!
(For Mayor Marion Berry)
11-10-1994 - 6:40 a.m.

D/Cs gone funky—
The man is in
And the lady's out,
it's time to cheer
Time to jump N SHOUT
Takes courage to come back,
But trust in God,
Don't give in
You're sure to win,
And now that it's over
And you've won again—
Thank God for winning
But forget not your friends.
Forward and upward—
We're proud of you, man
And our soul and eyes
Will watch you rise
So be-the-hero-you-are,
Be our African Star—
Stay on the case
And remember your race!

Could'nt Write a Poem For Mama

I tried to write
a poem for your birthday
Expressing what
I feel for you
on another milestone

I tried to think
of something that
I had not written,
or said, or done
to demonstrate
how a proud son
really felt about his mother

I tried to put words together
because I'm good at making rhyme
I even tried to think—up
some kind of new jingle structure
to impress you
with my poetic brilliance

I tried and tried
and thought and thought,
and imagined and dreamed
while riding that awful bus
to Elizabeth City, North Carolina
But I didn't think of nothing
I did'nt imagine nothing
and I did'nt dream of nothing

But I did feel
during intervals
of mind expansion
that it really was'nt necessary
to write a poem
or scribble a few jingles to say
what my heart knows,
That it's so wonderful
to have a mother
as sweet, as creative, and
as inspiring as you.

So I put my pen
back in my shirt pocket
folded-up the paper
that the man
gave me at the last bus stop
put it in my pants pocket
and went on back
to dreamland
feeling good all over.
Any how—
Happy Birthday/Mother Dear!

I WILL Say-it:
"Happy Birthday, April"
(To her memory)
April 6, 1993 - 10:50 p.m.

Not all the verses by Paul Laurence Dunbar—
    or Langston Hughes;
Not all the tapping by Bo Jangles—
    Or Sammy Davis, Jr.;
Not all the music by Scott Joplin—
    Or Duke Ellington;
Not all the drama by Paul Robeson—
    Or William Warfield;
Not all the novels by Alice Walker—
    or Toni Morrison;
Not all the songs by Sarah Vaughn—
    or Billy Eckstein;
Not all the raps by Ice Tea—
    or H. Rap Brown;
Not all the plays by Ameer Baraka—
    or James Baldwin;
Not all the poems by Nikki Giovanni—
    or Sonia Sanchez.
Not all the essays by W.E.B. DuBois—
    or Booker T. Washington;
Not all the dialogues by Kwame Toure—
    or Malcolm X;
Not all the gospel by Mahalia Jackson—
    or Sister Rosetta Thorpe;
Not all the baseball by Willie Mays
    All the duets by Sam and Dave
    All the speeches by Benjamin Mays,
Can say/ "Happy Birthday," like I will,
To A/prIL! "HAPPY BIRTHDAY, APRIL"

(Incidentally, when I went by her job to give her
the above poem, she was dead. This means that
she died without ever having read this poem.)

Just You & Me
10-7-90 - 2:35 p.m.

UNI spells unity/Cause—
No-telling
              What we'll do
together/nobody knows
Much as everybody/does
they say,
The tree may grow high
Up-in-the sky in Brooklyn;
But roots lay in the earth.
Birds fly much better
When the wind is right
Fish swim in the water—
WITH the stream.
An umbilical cord severed
And a baby cries.
Mary AND Joseph
Jesus AND his disciples.
Allah sent Muhammad
And God made man—
For just you and me,
We dePEND on man/
For/ U-nity;
We need our Queens, too
For/HAR-mony.
We need-them both
        For you & me—
                Harambee!

Hang On In There, Shorty
(For my baby daughter, "Candy")
3-12-1996 - 8:45 p.m.

Hope's very important
And we ought to cling to it
No matter what.
Faith in that "hope's"
Also important.
Together they equal success,
But what about those
who've lost hope
those of little faith
How do they cope,
How do they make out?
Some call it stamina
other's sticktoitiveness
while others say it's perseverance.
There is another way, however—
     When you're burdened down
     and you feel like you've lost
     Your very best friend
     when hope is gone
     and your faith is waning
     and you've hardly enough strength
     to make it through the night;
Hang-on-in-there ba-BY
Hang-on-in-there ba-BY
     When no matter how hard
     You pray
     your troubles appear again
     and again
     each and every day
     Hang-on-in-there ba-BY
     And later on when the stars
     shine beyond the rainbow
     and you look back

and see the hell hounds
on your track
and wonder how you got over
Maybe—just maybe
You'll really know
the importance of the phrase—
Hang-on-in-there ba-BY
Hang-on-in-there ba-BY!
Hang on—
No matter what!

This and That
April 2, 1994 - 11:41 a.m.

This is what I desire on a daily basis
Twenty-four seven
This is what I must remember
each and every day in every way
This is what I must practice
At all times in my mind
This is what I must pray for
365/66 days and nights per year
This is what I must realize
eternally, forever and never forget—
That I need patience
That I need tolerance
That I need humility
That I need honesty
That I need a forgiving heart
Always.

I Believe

Written on the eve of the historic moon landing
July 19, 1969

Man's going to the Moon
I don't care who's there!
He's bent on getting
This world somewhere
And Moon people green
Who live up there
WANT those brave earthlings to get somewhere.

And it won't be long
and they'll return to us!
With more knowledge gained
And maybe Moondust.

Guess Doubting Thomas
No longer will deceive
He'll eat his hat
And now believe
That scientific truths
Will never deceive.
Progress will continue and this I believe!

Anonymity
(For my buddy, Tommy—deceased)
May 12, 1989

And so Yo/boy got clean,
Stopped using EVERYTHING
And got real busy recovering and
I was sorta glad, myself—
I welcomed Yo—and in the
next eighty days or more
Yo did everything we told-him
To do.

He sat on the front row and kept
His mouth shut and kept that thing
Out of his neck. Yo was real cool, you know!
In the meanwhile, Yo got a job
At the same corporation where I worked.

One afternoon, after Yo had gotten
His ninety day key chain
He was riding in his pretty yellow truck
In the area where my office was
And where all the executives and dignitaries
Were constantly passing by—
Yo must have seen me getting ready
To go up the steps to say something
To my boss, who, by the way
Was not an addict—

Suddenly, I heard this loud noise
And rumbling sound—You guessed it!
it was Yo. Yo had put on brakes
So hard—(screech, screech), that
The truck had come to a halt
Abruptly—and all of the debris
in the back of the truck had pushed

Toward the front including Yo's tools
Work clothes and everything else—

Wham-a-lam-bam-God damn—
That was the sound it made!
At the same time, almost simultaneously,
Yo had seen me and jumped out
Of his truck doing flips
Three somersaults and the butterfly

At the same time! When Yo reached
Me he threw both arms around my
Back and neck—almost squeezing me
To death and saying—keep coming back,
Yo—how you feel, Brother Man? After
I dusted myself off and sort of regained
A little consciousness of what in the
Hell was going on, I assured Yo
That everything was just fine, but
Yo just had to shake my hand anyway;
And he damn near broke it!

When Yo returned to his truck through
That cloud of dust he had caused, and
Before he climbed back in—
Yo extended both hands in the air
And reminded me in a roaring voice—
There's an N.A. meeting tonight.
By that time I had forgotten all about
My boss/man and said just as loud
To Yo: "More will be revealed, Yo,
Keep Coming Back, More Will Be Revealed"

Light and Love
October 19, 1990, 7:58 a.m.

In search of
                light
I investigated
                love
        Looking for the answer!
Then I touched
                the sun
                with my face
And never a trace
                Of war or hate.
I was in-the-right-
        Love IS light.

The More Things Change?

From: "Brother can you spare a dime?"
        Year, 1930

To: "I'm homeless"
        "I'm blind"
        "I'm deaf"
        "I'm a veteran"
        "I work for food"—
                Year 1997.

What-up for the year 2000"

PEACE AT LAST
January 22, 1991 - 12:00 noon

The end of the day
    When it's time to lay
This tired body down;
When the sun
    Has disappeared
And the moons in the skies
    Are on the rise;
When darkness decides
    To fill the light—
I know it's al/right
Because I have finished my task
    And have not asked
To/be treated more or less than
    any man.
Then after day's end
    And night begins,
I settle back
    For a long sleep
In my Master's soul to/keep.
In these final hours
    I hold the power
To at-last complete
    My mission
In grateful submission
To a newly found work—
    A serenity, for
    an eternity!

A Black Shinning Light
Tribute to the late George James, and
Drs. John Henrik Clarke; Ron Karenga,
and Molefi Asanta
Dedicated to all my students—then and
now—whom I have loved and love so
dearly and sincerely

In these times of darkness and fear
It is refreshing to know that
Shinning lights DO appear
when they are needed.
John Henrik shines brightly
Today (thank God for the others too),
It's going to be the African way/
in the community.
Thanks to Clarke
We now embark—on the road to truth.

    <u>Not Out of Africa</u>, a phrase—a book
not to enlighten
but to frighten;
    Written to enslave
    For the mess THEY'VE made—
those so-called European scholars
like Mary Leskovitch
and the rest of those—yeah!
Un-huh!
    The European debate, which comes of late,
    Is about the fate, of the African past
    How long will it last;
that history of the ancient world,
It's about Africa's place and its Black face—
in it; it's about
    the bell curve, which pinches my nerve
    (Yours too, I hope.)
And the shaky <u>Black Anthena</u>
and all the other subtleties of 21 st century racism.

Yes, its revealed again,
          much to my chagrin—
Their racist attacks on
          Africa
          But there is one who stands
          out above the rest,
Who seems to be the lone warrior
In his rejections of the rejectors—
Clarke knows that the middle east, afar
          is really Northeast Afri-KA;
and that European history, really began
about 10,000 yrs after Africa's did!

Accolades for Clarke—James and Asanta
who make us all
A little taller in our knowledge
of the Pearl of the World—
Ake-bu-land.

REAGAN COUNTRY
8-12-1996

I been hanging out lately
Hearing me some things—
Like I hear a lot 'bout, well—
Ronald, proposition 13, against
affirmative action, snuff dipping,
No movie playing,—REAGAN!
I hear the G. O.P.'s still his party—
every part of it.
I hear it's ReaGun's agenda
that still drives America.
My, my
That's why we can't get no damn where!
And I thought he was sick?
WELL—

For My Students Here and There
Yesterday and Tomorrow
9-7-1996; 7:21 p.m.
(Dedicated to my students
everywhere in the universe)

For my students from GED to Ph.D.;
From Sarasota, Florida; Eatonton, Georgia;
Durham, North Carolina; Columbus, Ohio;
Carbondale, Illinois; Des Moines, Iowa;
Jefferson City, Missouri; and
from Ypsilanti, Michigan;
New York City to Baltimore, Maryland—
I thank God for the privilege/of
sitting on the edge/of
the 21 st century—
contemplating the mysteries/of
time and space.
I have complete faith
in this generation of students
They can and will master
change.
These young folk
These cosmopolites
These renaissance people
Who have traveled around the world
to Africa
to the Caribbean
To Paris and Vienna, Switzerland and Holland,
To New York City and Atlanta, Georgia
to the Nile and the Yangtze
to the Andes and Mt. Everest
to Tokyo
to London
Yes, and even to outer space—
These young people

who have worn their jeans
their gold chains, their cowrie shells—
beads and one ear ring
rastafari hair (locked) and bleached
hair and curled hair and braided hair
and silk stockings and no stockings;
These young people
who have demonstrated for causes
in which they believed
participated in the Million Man March
and the Million Woman March
and the Million Youth March
These young people
are not resistant to change
and rapid change—in this computer
internet age—is what they know
best and can master best.
And as for my few years—beautiful years
when I have been with them—
Yesterday and today
I have merely been
a part of a godly company—
I have never traveled the high road
alone. And now in my retirement
I shall always have their memory
with me—a memory
my very own!

Me and My Man, Dunbar

Unlike my man, Dunbar
Some folk just flat-out
like ta
      sit around the house
smok/
      in
a pipe and pitching logs
      in the fireplace.

They like ta
      sit outside
on the porch
      in the swing
bathing in Mother Nature—
      watching the bluebird,
      becoming intoxicated
with the landscape—
      the scent of a rose
the touch of the wind
      or the smile of the sun.

There are other people
      Who like sit'n
      on a river/
          bank
watching the ball and tackle sink
and then pulling up on a perch or a blue gill
or a bluefish or a robin or a croaker,
or just hauling in
a bunch of crabs;
      and then there're
these other folk
      like me
Oh yeah!
      They stay / up

late at night/
      real late!
They just sit around the house/
      for a minute
watching TV—
      sometimes even
      taking the trash out
      walking the dog,
maybe sitting on the steps
      for about a micro second,
But really/
      "for real, for real"—
deep down in their souls
      there are "street people"
      who like to just hangout/
      Stayout—(as a matter of fact)
standing on street corners
and closing bars
      or the church—
wherever the people are?/The excitement's
      the street, man, yeah—
      the streets!

That's their forte.

They get their kicks
      watching the sun
      coming up over the horizon,
      or the moon
      over the mountains,—
walking down Fifth Avenue
      3 O'clock in the morning
      eating pizza pies.

They like the midnight night smells,
the whore's yells
to the "tricks"
for a fix, you know—
They like to watch crap games
in the alley.
And chess in the barber shop—
the cop on the beat
the bum in the street,
Wherever the "street" is
that's where these folks are,

But really—
We're all, different
You know—like—
"different strokes for different folks?" ha,
Or like when my man, Paul, wrote
in his own little dialect, "I'm just an Easy Going
Fellow"
(I think it's time to end all this). Besides,
I forgot all about My Man
Dunbar?

Listen Up!

A Street Killing on Greenmount Avenue in July 1998,
Baltimore, Maryland.

Written July 19, 1998

We need some prayer—
Up in here,
Some fun, but not the gun
A bit of hope, but not the dope,
Lots of love, from above
Let's end the hate, and get things straight

instead of:

Victims pleading
Nobody heeding
Squad cars speeding
Yo/ boy bleeding
Hustlers selling,
Sniches is telling;
Seems to be,

for you and me—

No stopping to copping./
   chilling and killing—
Rapping and stopping to buy dope and coke
from big wheelers and dealers,
And then to die face down
on the ground
with folks all around
         starring and crying
on the streets of the city
what a pity—
So young, so gifted, So Black—
And on crack?
Listen up Yo, listen up Mr. Man
Can you hear the the messages of my mind
Umph.
Can you hear the Healing of my mind
Uh-huh— yeah.
Listen up man— uh-huh
                  yeah.

Listen Up!

Is William Jefferson The "New Nigger"?
9-28-1998
12:45 p.m.

I had some misgiving
And a whole/ lot of hostility
For him at first—
'Cause it looked like
It was just another Red/Neck
In office
And so far as I was concerned
Had'nt Nut-ing changed!
But here lately,
Since he AND his saxophone
Have got into a big mess
Over when and where
He ought to be
Jumping up on, or in a female;
I sorta have been changing
My mind.
I guess it all came clear
When I discovered
That New Gingrich— all the conservatives
Plus Russ-aw-w whatever his name is
Had lined/up against Mr. William;
And that he was now catering
To females and African Americans.
I said: "Lordsy me?" My man
Has finally learned some sense—
And so I'm casting my little vote
For William Jefferson Clinton
In whatever elections I can.
(And all the other "Clinton" people.)

146

Africa
January 25, 1995; 6:45 a.m.

The beginning, the world
Where it all unfurled, the Melanin
The land, the forest the desert's
Dusty face. Deep down in the womb
Is the conception of an amazing people,
A dark people, a Pygmy people
A Watussi people, an enslaved people
Who would heal the land, make the blind to see;
Who heal nations and churches
Make great contributions discover
Firsts and invent first and accomplish firsts
And then make something out of nothing—
Africa immortal— one of a kind.

THEN ALONG CAME HARRIET

(For The Former Vice President
of Morgan State University:
Dr. Harriet Trader)

Every now and then I get to feeling
Sorry for myself, perhaps, because
I didn't become a James Baldwin
Or a Charlie "Yardbird" Parker,
A Ben Chavis or Charles Wesley—
And began to blame it all on inferiority
And academic defects and then along comes
A person like Dr. Trader— for whom I have profound
Respect, and deep admiration—to say Just
The right thing at the right time. And that's when
My self esteem rises to the level it should
Have never left; and I feel good all over again.
I thank you for the kind remarks, Doc, I shall never
Forget them nor you. May the muse always send a
"Harriet Trader" around at just the right time!

For Them

We build institutions,
And light our pathways
With torches of where we were, and
Acquire new knowledge of self,
And create new ways
To express our Unity and love for each other
In order to
Press forward through life's raging storms—
Discovering revelations
And innovations never/ever realized
Were true.
We have done all this,
And we will do even greater things
For him, to win, and
For them to begin—
Our boys and girls of the sun
Who look to one
Like us to lead them
Out of the pits of ignorance
Into the sunlight of truth and justice.

On the Passing of My Friend
From Childhood Days,
Mr. James Williams, Musician
**Died on Saturday, March 4, 1995; Funeral Held
at Rivers Morgan Funeral Parlor, 701 West Street,
New Bern, North Carolina,
March 7, 1995 at 12:35p.m.**

When I heard the news last night
That my friend had passed on
I cried for about a minute
Then I moved on; For we had shared
Some great moments together, James and I,
Even intimate ones. We had done
Some great things together in music
Under some great Band directors—
Leon Mizell, Percy Jenkins, R. Hayes Strider,
And had blown together
With some great musicians—
Zack Green, Charlie Keller, Grandy Tate
Sticks Darden, Robert Poole
And so many others. Boy! We had a ball,
You Know, I remember those weekends
We played at Club Cario in Baltimore
And Dr. Edward's Medicine show,
In Fairmont, North Carolina,
And at the 65 club in Jacksonville, N.C.
And the marching bands in Washington, D.C.
and New York and in the Zanzibar and Club 102
in New Bern
And that time we went on the road
With "Sonny Boy" Williams, and
Silas Green and Bardex and the Florida Blossoms
And Kaus' shows—
So many memories, and they are all good
So this is no time to cry
It's time to say goodbye—
To one of the greatest musicians
In my past, James Williams—
A Musician's musician.
So long, James;"
I'll be seeing you..."

What Goes Around
Comes Around

      Bitching
Was Yo/boy's first name.
He had been in the joint
Practically all his life
And all his life, he complained
Bout everything
But when he got out
He did the same ole thing
Over and Over again
And expected different results.
That great day was here, again!
Yo/boy had been anticipating
This day for eighteen months and
He was esctatic—wild with joy and
Ready to go
Get laid or get paid; it didn't much matter which;
And so the night before
Yo/boy could barely sleep.
He began to shake and shiver
And walk the "flo"
And like, Wow!
As a matter of fact
Yo/boy had just done
Telling his boys that he wanted to leave yesterday;
That he wanted to catch that Night Train
already gone. They thought it rather funny
But Yo/boy was dead serious.
Yo/boy stopped talking about 9 am
That morning, and when he started up
Again he was bitching 'bout
"He didn't belong in prison, nohow;"
And "about his mom
And sister and girlfriend
Who didn't get to see him
last Xmas Eve."

12:10, yo/boy was uptown
Sippin on a Near Beer"? Cause like
Yo had already promised the Lord
And all his Angelic host that if he ever
Got out this time he'd never, ever
Drug or drink again!
Anyway—by 12:20 yo had met
His old rap/buddy, —street doctor
And advisor.
At 12:30, yo was in the highrise
with a pipe full of smoke
A pocket full of dope
And a nose full of coke;
Yo was "ready for Freddie OR BETTY!
By one o'clock, yo/boy was right;
where he was an hour ago—in jail
Talking 'bout "how the system
Had done him wrong;" "If only
That white man would get off his neck?"
And "how he had received bad breaks
All his life."
Finally, Yo/boy exclaimed to the world:
        "Hey "Yo", if it don't be for bad luck
        I wouldn't have no luck at all!"
Yo was back Home—Again, prison—
Bitching!

Just Like That
2:45 a.m.

I saw that spanish boy
With his straight hair N' stuff
And I remembered when I wanted to/be
Just like that
Until I realized that
I was all I had
Which was a thing of beauty
All by-it/self.

Piano Man
6-26-1998; 5:00 p.m.

Dedicated to the <u>Afro</u> <u>American</u> Newspaper's
celebration of Black Music Month, June, 1998—
an original Poem

I play the piano, see— I'm universal.
That's what I say; but my
friends
say something else; they say
I'm Top Cat— Dynamite
" Saying Something," No I, and
the best damn Black piano player in the
world of music. I don't say that!
I say simply— I am
a
Piano
Man— a pianist, if you will.
I'm not satisfied with playing like Count
Basie
Earl Garner or the Duke.
I am not especially eager to play like
Scott Joplin, Theolonious Monk or
Fats Waller;
I get no kicks from imitating
Samuel Coolridge Taylor, Jelly Roll
Morton
      William Grant Still or James A. Bland ?
I wanna be a Key Board Virtuoso, not a
Black Virtuoso
I wanna play the dazzling transcriptions of Frank
Churchhills'
delightful—Reminiscences of Snow White,
Gershwin's Rhapsody in Blue.
I want to be remembered for the echoes

you hear in my music from
Padereski and Rochmaninof and Josef
Hofmann.
I want you to marvel at the way
I play
Lizst and Chopin and Beethoven;
For I'm not just a Black Piano
Man
I'm a cosmopolite— a man of the diaspora
and I want to play like Johann
Strauss, too, and
Bach, and emulate the virtuosity in Handel's
Messiah
or give renditions like Leopold Godowsky or even Earl
Wild
I don't care?
I just want all of you to know
I am not a Black Piano Man—
I am a Piano Man for all the world and all
the people to/hear.

To A Southern Lady

(For Juanita)
August 23, 1998
2:30 A.M.

The first time
      I saw her—
That is— really saw her
I envisioned Magnolia trees
And sunflowers; peach blossoms
Daffodils and homemade ice-cream,
Linen dressers and hominy girts—
Cotton candy and honeysuckers and grapevines;
Oh, how I delighted in
The fond recall of home," The Southland,"
It dazzled me!
The next time I saw her
My imagination soared again;
Only with this time

I realized a deeper meaning
of a word.
I came up with—
"Vivid,"
Yet that word never, really came to me
Until I saw her that second time,
And it came so suddenly
And so clear

I was transfigured, and
I almost yelled out—
Yeah!
I saw her, now, as just being plain—
Without any pretense or phony mannerisms—
Just her sassy, southern self
She seemed to encompass the very essence
Of simplicity— and yet
She remained jovial, uncomplicated
Witty and sharp; but what attracted me most
I guess, was that Southern charm
And that certain manner of speaking
I had grown
So accustomed to seeing and hearing
In the Old South before I left.
And what's more—
She even stepped with Southern dignity
Without any of the urban influences
Southerners
Seem to pick up on whenever we
Come North— you know, "putting-on"
And the like. To me
She symbolized a kind of "Southern
Black woman"
Very rarely seen or heard of
In Northern parts nowadays,
Especially if one is from the South.
I shall always remember her, kindly.

Rosa Parks

The first time
I saw her—
the first time
I saw her-face in Detroit;
her long grey hair
tied around-her-head
like a rope
Her two-piece
brown, tweed pleated-skirt
and turtle/neck little sweater
with her arms folded
while sitting-up-straight;
Now and then a smile
on her petit brown face
looking ahead through her glasses—
Then my eyes dropped down
to her feet—
legs/crossed at the bottom
those tired feet
that began it/all
way-back in Alabama
making it possible
for all-of-us
to walk taller
ride better
and have/a bit more faith.
The first time
I saw her/
the first time
I saw her-face in Detroit
I knew the meaning
of feet being tired
but soul rested!

A DEDICATION FOR YOUNG BLACK STREET MEN IN THE CITY OF BALTIMORE
Just You and Me Black Heritage Program
WEAA 88.9. Sunday, 9-10 pm

This program is dedicated to smartly
Dressed Black men who wear bow ties and sell
Bean Pies and newspapers on North Avenue
And Edmondson Avenue and Greenmount Avenue
And York Road, and downtown, and uptown
And crosstown, and "round town" in Baltimore City;
This program is dedicated to that group of
Young men who do not commit violence
In the street, on street corners
And in vacant lots, and who respect their elders.
This program is dedicated to that group
Who make the neighborhoods safe;
Who secures and protects projects and grocery
Stores and churches and community stores
And organizations and corporations
So that old folk like me—and young folk like you—can
    walk
The streets of Baltimore safely without fear and the
    threat
of drive-by shootings; drug wars and personal attacks,
This program is dedicated to that group of young
    Black men
Who do not rape our young women
Commit mayhem, abuse their children
And my children, and our children.
This program is dedicated to that group of young
    Black men
Who do not beat up on their wives or their mothers
or fathers; and who support family
Uplift and African Heritage on a daily basis
I dedicate this program to these street men
These well mannered, gentlemen; these
    knowledgeable
And   aware street men of color and of dignity
And   worth in the highest order—
        Keep it up—young—Black—African men,
           African Soldiers
        Keep it up—get stronger Black Man, Keep it
up.—
        Bring US—T O G E T H E R.

ME 'n GRANDMA

Back during the depression
when we lived in Brooklyn
with Grandma—or John
she liked to/be called
since she belonged to Father Divine-
Grandma always took-up the slack for Mama.
One sad/day morning when
Grandma did/nt wan-a-wake/up Mama
I tip-toed
to the kitchen
where Grandma
chewed/up some carrots
and made me eat 'em
Fore I could protest/
meanwhile—mama turned over
and snowed
like she always did early in the morning
as I slid pass her
edging my way
through the bedroom furniture
to the hallway
where I tripped/over
the train
my Mama bought me for xmas
Then we caught the trolley
to Chinatown,
where Grandma bought me
the prettiest pair of shoes
I ever did see.
They say Blk/folks
wuz doing pretty bad
during depression time,
but dem shoes,—
my Grandma bought
wuz alright by me!

A Tree Grows in Ghana

For (Dr. Patricia Newton)
Dedicated to the sainted memory of my beloved, Dr.
John Henrik Clarke, a historian and an attacker of
myths about the history and culture of African peoples
in the Diaspora

August 9, 1998; 11:30 p.m.

Somewhere
A tree stands in Africa
and it's bark
Is Clarke,

The story begins, but never will it end;
For the tree grows, as the African child grows—
always defending, never ending
The glory—
Oh, let us hear the story
of the tree,
they planted for me!

Yes, now grows a tree
in the nation of Ghana!
In the Black soil of the Mother Land
Rising up through the muck and mire
of the chains and strain
and shame
of the bloody slave trade
Grows, green, the limbs and leaves
of freedom's son and heir
to African liberty— and
His name: Dr. John Henrik Clarke.

Alas! For him that tree grows
     to bear his name
     and claim to fame,
Causing us to honor him
With our continuance
     in the struggle for liberation
     for Black folk everywhere
     in the diaspoRA—
Yes, a tree grows in GhaNA.
In the midst of nationhood and development
       it grows in truth and integrity
        worth and dignity;
       it grows in love and justice and
May its bough always
Stretch out its lofty hands unto God
And may it always recall

    the ancient prophecy of the sage:
"Princes shall come out of Egypt
Ethiopia shall soon spread out
her wings unto God."
And now as we sing the new songs
     of hope and joy
     for the coming new century
Let us always remember the good
John Henrik Clarke

    and Marcus Garvey
    and Authur Schomberg
    and J.A. Rogers
    and Drusilla Dungee
    and Anta Diop
    and John Jackson
    and Queen Nzinga, too.

Strong And Mighty Man
(In memory of the late St. Patrick Nelson)

I'm a/ man, a Phenomenal" MAN—
Strong, Black standing tall
Amid the strife, in life—
Turning right and walking straight,
Never leaning, never falling—
Brother Black man
That's me.

I build corporations, stable relationships,
Bring U-ni-ty, to the comm-ni-ty
Brother Black man, mighty
Afri-Kan— Black
Strong Black man
That's me.
I don't walk, I glide in my stride
I prance, dance— tiptoe, arrogantly.
My gait is gallant
My eyes looking up
I am proud, in appearance
My shoes tired— shirt buttoned
on straight, pants pulled up
I feel good and I look good
I can do want I want to do
I can be what I want to be

Strong and mighty Black man
Free—
That's ME!

Coming On Up
From Ohio State University

(I can — See the Pyramids along the Nile/)
Yesterday
I stood beside the enchanted Nile
and marveled
at the mystery of the sphinx.
I saw the beauty of the desert
greeted the rising Sun
and bowed in solemn worship.
I wandered
through Africa's torrid forest and
sat in awe before the bamboo huts —
walked beside the Nile's sacred shores
stopped at Timbuktu
and felt her spirit of destiny
vibrate through my being.

(I can — See the pyramids along the Nile/)
I chanted the songs
of unknown bards and troubadours
studied strange philosophies
watched Mother Africa
Pat Pythagoras' head, and
rock Socrates, Plato, and Aristotle to sleep
in her cradle of knowledge/
I starved and hungered
on the Middle Passage—
felt the whips and scorns, the
hypocrisy, injustice—
the curse of racism and enslavement/

(I can — See the Pyramids along the Nile/)
As a slave
I learned to hate and dream
resist and run— I
felt the strap
cutting into my quivering flesh;
and my blood
rushing to the hot gaping wounds.
Yes, I know the agony
of sweat and toil — the bondage
that men and women endure—
in what they think and feel/
I know the subtlety, the charm
the guile, the wit
the games— the laughter
that colored my actions
against that awful oppression/
(Yes,— I can see the Pyramids along the Nile/)
Today
I feel the herald
of a New Awakening—
the presence of a new soul
I hear the trumpet of a New Day
to see —
AFRICA!
And it belongs to ME;
for I remember— And
I can still — See the Pyramids along the Nile!

AND THEN CAME N'ALBINO

(For Ahoski, North Carolina)

We wuz roll'n alon' singing
Some song, doing nothing wrong
Then came n' albino
Who wuz a wino.
He wanted some smackn'
We did'nt give no slack
Until we heard a crack
That he wuz n Albino
And a stone wino.
Til' that time, we wuz
Doing fine, drinking our wine
But we met n' Albino
Who wuz too, a wino.
He started stiffin' n'jivin,
Lying but buying
SO we accepted the Albino
Who wuz really a wino.
From that point on he had
Us conned, and a snicher warned
That this wasn't no Albino
And surely no wino.
It didn't take long, before
OPur stuff wuz in pawn, and our freedom gone
Where in hell is that Albino
Who wuz a wino.
Man he sho split quick

When in came the Dick cross
Our heads wid his stick
But he looked like the Albino
Who wuz really the wino.
When our heads cleared up
N' we filled our cap
We wuz down on our luck
Then along came the wino
That we thought was an Albino.
He took us to jail
Whipped our tail tired
His best to send us to hell
That damb Albino
Who wasn't never no goddamn wino.
Lord-dee as long as the eyes can see
Don't ever show no Albino
To me
Especially
If he's n' Albino
Who really ain't no wino.

Communication
2-9-96, 12:05 p.m.

I got off the plane
>   and walked down
>   the runway
to the entrance
>   where she stood
>   with both hands on her hips
>   shaking profusely. When she saw me
she quickly rolled her eyes on
to both sides simultaneously
>   and folded those black painted
brown eyelids—
>   those big-wide eye pupils
of hers, and then she
>   immediately opened them;
>   and we both knew that it was
>   THAT TIME—
and so we split quick!
And that was the best move
I ever did make
>   in all my life./
We made beautiful love.

Understanding
8-11-1998; 8:55 p.m.

I don't know why
I never thought of it,
It seemed easy enough
But it never ever—
really came to my mind.
Maybe it was because of its simplicity?
God knows we said it enough,
But it just didn't seemed to fit;
I couldn't comprehend it at all
until that last time I went out
and that ole devil caught up
with me again. It was then
When I got that last whipping
That my devastation reached
An all time low
And I was about ready to
Kill myself or somebody else that
It came to me; and this time
It was so clear
That a blind man could see it.
It went like this,
And I understood it well that time:
"If you don't put it in you,
you can't get High."

MO
May 12,1989

Mo really had-it to/gether. Just out of jail ,
Mo knew everything; had done everything
Could recite the Rubaiyat at the Torah
charming incantations and knew the Koran
                              Backward
Mo was alright
Mo knew Ju-gyps-su, con-fu

                              And could boggaloo

Mo was bad—real bad. Mo knew Arabic
Swahi-li and could find Kansas Ci-ty /

                              On the map
Mo was alright,
Mo could locate ancient Asia
                              Medieval Rome
And Nome, Alaska.
Mo was alright
Mo could preach, teach,
                    Play checkers
And chess the best.
Mo faced the East three time a day.
Didn't eat no pork and he horned his past
By going on a fast
Mo could do everything
                    'cept
Keep that "thing"
                    Out of his neck:
BUt Mo was all-l-l-l-RIGHT!

Greenmount and North

Across the tracks
        To a Relationship
Only understood
        By the Bloods
In the Hood—
            HOME!

The Music Goes Round And Round...?

Looks like
all our young men
like to do now
is sell dope
buy pretty, expensive clothes
sold and made by white folks,
go to jail
talk about Black Heritage
get religion
practice law
come home
sell more dope
go back to jail
talk about Black Heritage
get religion
practice law
come home
sell more—well ?

171

JAMIE

written especially for Jamie, age 8
June 23,1998 12:50 noon

God's got his eyes on you, child—
Daddy's little girl,
and HE's gonna see you through
all the storms of life
by way of your mother's loving attention
to the smallest of your needs.
God's got his hands on you, girl—
little one
full of fun;
and mommie and daddy
are counting on you
to "come through," too.
So be good. Study hard like you should.
Be the sun in the rainbow
Be the star in the sky;
Be excellent, be brilliant
Be GREAT before you die!

Funerals

A whole bunch of young folks—
Sisters and brothers were standing around
The Funeral Parlor the other day
Looking strange and acting peculiar
Starring into space, perhaps wondering
Who's gonna get shot next,
Who's going to get the next "package"
And when will the killing stop.
Funny how the same brothers and sisters
Doing all the killing are the same ones
Doing all the whooping and crying
At and around the Funeral Parlor.
And there's another group, talking about
Revenge and "let's give the family something."
Of course the family never gets anything
But that's okay.
In fact the family is too busy getting high
Themselves. They would'nt have time to be
Gett'n paid anyway.
In the meanwhile—
Hearses move slow—cause they got
No place to go—but the Funeral Parlor!
And you can holler and wallow all
You want to—the brother won't come
Back. His "Brother" made sure of that—
One to the head and one to the chest
Made sure that the brother would'nt be
fit for nuthing but flowers and
tears and a whole lot of talk at the
Funeral—none of which will bring the
brother back,
Underneath the gilded atmosphere
of expensive cars, high priced tennis
Shoes and the latest style outfits, there's
a sac of woe at the funeral procession

Where young Black men and cute little
Sisters-congregate to see's who's
present and how they put the brother
away. And the brother IS sharp in
His suede casket and leather suit—but
he won't be getting up at the funeral
And saying: "ya'll," like he use to
Say or "I'm alright, Man." Wish
he could speak though, at least a
final word before he's off to eternity?
Perhaps he'd remind yo/boy
that "it's a one ticket deal!—only
One party at the Funeral Parlor, per-
lifetime!"
Yo/sisters better keep those "outfits ready"
Yo/boys better keep those tennis shoes clean
NO telling where the funeral's coming
Their way
All I know is that it will—
Yo/boys love; to kill —yo/boys;
And they love to sell dope, coke
Whatever, and count money.
That's the "way of yo/boys"
That's the yo/boys' blues.
That's the Funeral Parlor Blues.
By the way—
The rest of his "rap" buddies
Better look out
Cause right after the funeral
Somebody's looking for them
With a bullet carrying their names, too.
Incidentally—
There's a whole lot of family crying.
And grave-yard digging nowadays;
And it looks like there's gonna be
Plenty more "standing around" Funeral Parlors,
Looking strange and wondering
Where the next shot or hook/up
Is coming from?

New History

I want a new kind of history
    like Nat Turner, David Walker,
    Richard Wright, Langston Hughes,
    Claude McKay, James Baldwin, Fannie Lou
Hamer
I need a new history, now;
    A story that makes me visible
I need a new history;
    A story that Malcolm spoke to the grassroots
I need a new history;
    A story that Adam Clayton Powell preached
I need a new history;
    A story that H. Rap Brown told
I need a new history;
    A story that Kwame Toure screamed
I need a new history;
    A story that Minister Farakhan recommends
I need a new history;
    A story that Frances Kress Welsing informs
I need a new history;
    A story that Mary McCloud Bethune willed
I need a new history;
    A story that Na'im Akbar suggests
I need a new history;
    A story that Ivan Van Sertima discovered
I need a new history;
    A story that John Henrik Clark told
I need a new history;
    A story that Earl E. Thorpe taught
I want a new kind of history;
    History like Margaret Walker, Shirley
    Chisholm, Dr. Helen Edmonds, Sonia Sanchez,
    Drusilla Dungee, Dr. Samuel Banks, Dr. Jesse
    McDade, Congressman Kweisi Mfume, Dr.
    Yousef Ben Jochannan, Franz Fannon, C.L.R.
    James, Tony Brown, Na'im Akbar - **Black Rage**
    and **Jesus Bag**--Benjamin Chavis;

I want a new kind of Black History;
      Like Angela Davis, Rev. Al Sharpton, Vincent
      Harding, Maulana Ron Karenga, Randall
      Robinson, Rosa Parks, Khalid Muhammad,
      Louis Farrakhan
I want a new history;
      A new kind of commitment
      A new kind of awareness
      A new kind of president and mayor
      And governor and policemen and employers—
      And Congress
      And, most of all, "a brand new me"
I need a new history;
      A Sankofa kind of revelation
I need, I need, I need, I need, I need—yeah
I sho / nuff need
      A new history—man
      A new kind of real history
I want a new HISTORY!

Look What the Circus Did in Baltimore!
(For my friend Amy, thanks)
April 4,1993 6:45 p.m.

The circus is fun—it's for everyone.
Cotton and candy's just fine and dandy—
some hot-dogs and clowns
N' the merry go round;
And then/there's the "Game"
And you won't be the same/
When you leave the circus.
That's the way it use to be;
the circus meant glee
It meant acts and acrobats
Lion tamers and games
And midgets and giants
And jumping through fires
And walking on barb/wire.
I like flyers in the breeze
On the high trapeze.
Eating corn and French/fries
Apples and pies.
Trained seals—flapping their wings—
Dancing girls, and everything;
And the circus band's the best in the land.
That's the way it use to-be/
At least for me.
Something exciting, something weird;
But look at it now
What the circus did?
I can see the ELEPHANTS; even now
Between Eutaw and Paca at Lexington Street—
Lifting up their big brawny legs—
Yes/ cocking up their one/leg high in the sky
And making out of space noises
As they did their stuff (you know) business

It was funny, but painful, I mean
That smell, and God—that noise.
Waw—UMP, waw-w-UMP. "Damn it!
Shet/up—you big ole fat elephants. Ha!
Anyway—I just love to see the circus
Come to-town. And gee how I like
The animals like the lions and tigers
And monkeys and alligators and all.
And for-a- while, especially this year
I loved to/watch the elephants.
They are such graceful animals
Not at all how the movies often portrays
Them. But all of this changed a few days
Ago when they brought all of those elephants
In the parking lot downtown
To do their thing and smell/up
Half of Baltimore. But that might
Not have been too bad if hadn't a been
For all those horses in the area
With the PO-lice sit'n on top of em,
Riding like Hop-along and Buffaloe Bill.
There ought to be a law against horses
And elephants "doing their business"
Together. Hell— it's bad enough
With all those two/ton lbs. of elephant's
Meat. Just imagine if you will,
What they did— together in that parking
Lot No—just imagine what they did
To set back the Health Department in
Baltimore, lot alone the thousands of
Nostrils they sent away searching
For clean air. Dear God—save us
From the elephants, especially the horses
And elephants together. My, my.
Why couldn't those cops take their horses
Some-place-else. Ump. ump. ump. I'll never
Go to the circus again.
And I certainly don't want to see
No elephants any—more. And if I

Ever do see another policeman riding
On a horse, I think I'll turn into wild
Bill or Bronco Billy or anything else
To/make me silly and go on a Rodeo
Rampage and get rid of all that
Elephant dukie and horse manure
They left in Downtown Baltimore.

One Sunday Morning...
January 8, 1996 12:00 Noon

In the little 'ole country town
Where I come from, Sunday
Really meant something! I mean
Sunday was the day we looked
Forward to. Because not only did I
Get my "hoghead" (50 cents), but I
Got a chance to wear my best clothes.
In other words, it was show-off day I
The old bald headed preacher with his
Dark shades and Cadillac car would
Come riding up to the church, and afterwards
The sisters would go home and prepare
The ministers favorite meal—chicken !
And I do mean chicken— "Gospel Bird"
Cause like that old preacher would
Actually hum and pat his feet as
He would eat the last piece of chicken
Then he'd clear his throat and say:
" Well, sister, are we having any
Dessert today? What about that sweet potato
Pie??" And then he would proceed
To eat up all the pies and the cakes, too,
Yes, indeed, Sunday was something else,
Man, and I looked forward to it with wild anticipation.
I remember one Sunday morning
In a particular way. Sister Fannie had on her lumber
jacket
Her feathered top hat, her red dress and
Her high heeled sneakers-on. Sister
Fannie was step-in high this "moaning"!
High yellow Susie— with her hip shaking self
Came in white— from head to toe. She was chewing
That gum faster than brother Giz/ZART
was dipping snuff, Then came sister Say-de —
Decked out in a brand now pants suit—

Leathered down with a scarf and gloves to match;
And With all her fourteen little bad ass boys
With their caps turned sideways and pants down below to their
knees hanging loosely on their butts. In
Strutted the pastor, Dr. Hargraves
Whose sermon was: " What Did Thou Come
For." Sister Say-de was the first
To the mike. "Well preacher, I tell ya,
It's like this chere, I came to git these here
Bad ass children straightened out."
"Huh-UMHP" was Rev. Hargraves reply. Now there
  seemed
To be pandemonium and chaos about midway
Of the church. The commotion had attracted
A lot of the parishioners on the front pews
In the rear. What happened was that
Sister Suzie had turned somersaults
From the balcony and had landed on both
Feet with tambourine and all in her hand still
Clanging. Sister Suzie hadn't missed a beat
And she hurried up and informed
Dr. Hargraves that she had come
For that strumpet who had stolen
Her man. Dr. Hargraves' reply was the
Usual "Huh-UMPH."
Brother Giz/ZART didn't have much to say except
That he came to got some of that ole time
Religion that his grandmother had often told him
  about.
To this the minister changed pace
And said, rather boisterously, AMEN and
A—MAN. But before the shouting and
And clapping begun in response to the preacher,
Sister Fannie had leaped cross four pews
And taken the mike from the minister and had
Made Brother Giz/ZART sit down and
Shet his mouth. "Here's what I come for
Ya'll: I come to get rid of this chicken-

Stealing, double-dealing, Cadillac buying, Hamburg
hat wearing, hyeena grinning, bear-hugging
Money-counting committee
Assigning, non-appointment-keeping,
Yellow women jumping, preacher!
Rev. Hargraves began singing this time—
"Should Jesus Bear the Cross Alone and all the world
    go free;
" His Eye is On The Sparrow and I know He
Watches Me." After that, somebody
Began doing the "Holy Dance"—somebody else
Spoke in tongues and another Holy
Sunday morning had begun.
It was going to be another great Sunday
For God, in that old Ebeneezer Black church
In the South!

Index

About The Author

Gossie Harold Hudson
Distinguished Educator and Scholar

Gossie Harold Hudson, Professor of History at Morgan State University, Baltimore, Maryland, you are a poet, an embryonic playwright, a musician, a journalist, and editor, a talkshow host, a scholar, and a humanitarian. Beginning your academic career at Morgan State, you earned both the bachelors and masters degree from North Carolina Central University, Durham, North Carolina and the Ph.D. degree from Ohio State University. Of your poetry, the Chairperson of the National Political Congress of Black Women, Inc. says "The majesty of your poetic genius overwhelmed me as I read your powerful thoughts so lyrically expressed." To further demonstrate your gift as a poet, you have, at press, a volume titled *My Soul Sings: Poetry in Sparetime.* You are also a professional musician who has played the alto saxophone with major and minor bands throughout the nation. But poetry and music are your avocations.

You, Gossie Hudson, are a scholar. Your scholarship is reflected in your seven books: *Forward for Freedom, Abraham Lincoln and the Negro (1974); A Directory of Black Historians, Essays and Commentaries (1975); The Paul Laurence Dunbar Reader (1976); My Soul Sings (1999); A Biography of Paul Laurence Dunbar (1999); Abraham Lincoln, Blacks and The Civil War, with Special Reference to William Florville (1999); and My Favorite Dunbar Poems (1999).* You have also written more than seventy-five articles that have appeared in

187

books, journals, magazines, and newspapers. A distinguished Paul Laurence Dunbar scholar, you mounted a national symposium on Dunbar at Morgan State (in 1978) that was responsible for the reconstruction and re-evaluation of Dunbar that secured the poet immortality in the African-American literary canon. You were also instrumental in getting the U. S. Postal System to issue a stamp honoring the poet, and for a number of years, a small commentary by him was listed in the annual U.S. Postal Catalogue.

For over a decade, you have produced and hosted "Just You and Me: A Two-Way Talk Show" on WEAA-FM. This program has been invaluable in enlightening the Black community of our contributions to the world and our place in history as an African people. In addition to your scholarship and your creativity, you have labored tirelessly in the community developing a substance abuse program for children and counseling addicts in the State Prison System. Your awards and honors are far too extensive to catalogue here, but two that typify your scholarship and your service to the community are Towson State University's Distinguished Marylander Award and Governor William Donald Schaefer's Community Award.

Dr. Hudson, for your scholarship and for your many contributions to the Black community, the Middle-Atlantic Writers Association is pleased to present to you, its Distinguished Scholar Award.

— RALPH RECKLEY, SR.
MORGAN STATE UNIVERSITY

Note: On June 27, 1999, Dr. Hudson received the Doctor of Humane Letters Honorary Degree, conferred by Sojourner-Douglass College.